EIGHT IS GREAT

Grant Deger

Village Books and Paper Dreams Publishing
BELLINGHAM, WA

Copyright © 2018 by Grant Deger.

All rights reserved. No part of this publication may be reproduced, distributed or transmitted in any form or by any means, including photocopying, recording, or other electronic or mechanical methods, without the prior written permission of the publisher, except in the case of brief quotations embodied in critical reviews and certain other noncommercial uses permitted by copyright law. For permission requests, write to the publisher, addressed "Attention: Permissions Coordinator," at the address below.

Village Books and Paper Dreams Publishing
1200 11th Street
Bellingham, WA 98225
www.villagebooks.com

Book Layout ©2017 BookDesignTemplates.com

Ordering Information:
Quantity sales. Special discounts are available on quantity purchases by corporations, associations, and others. For details, contact the "Special Sales Department" at the address above.

Eight is Great/ Grant Deger. -- 1st ed.
ISBN 978-0-6921855-4-4
LCCN 2018911445

To Family

Family is Nature's choice for mutual care, education, love, protection, and support. Family instills motivation, boundaries, and conscience.

Success is picking a good father and a good mother and starting your life in Ohio.
> —WILBUR WRIGHT

The next thing most like living one's life over again seems to be a recollection of that life, and to make that recollection as durable as possible by putting it down in writing.
> —BENJAMIN FRANKLIN

Don't do cocaine. Don't race trains. And avoid AIDS situations.
> — CHARLIE MUNGER (WARREN BUFFETT'S BUSINESS PARTNER)

Honor Thy Father and Thy Mother.
> —GOD

Contents

Introduction 1

The Book of Grant

Where The "Eight" Came From—Basic Genealogy 5
In the Beginning 27
Our First Home 29
World War II 33
Corpus Christi Grade School 37
Our Second Home 47
B-B guns 52
Radio, TV, and Telephones 53
Our Third Home 63
Chaminade High School 65
University of Dayton 73
Why Washington State? 77
The Brothers Three on Tour 78
Goodbye Blest Mother 91

The Book of Ron

The Begots 97
The "Peach" 113
Grade School 116
Newsboy 123
High School 125
Jobs 128
Fun Times 129

Automotive Adventures 131
College 132
Marine Corps and Marriage 136
Ron's Speech to the Chaminade Alumni Panel 137
Life in Dayton in the 1950s 138
Addendum 143

Stories by Rob, Chris, Paula, Beth, Phil, and Doug
Rob's Story 147
Chris's Story 150
Paula's Story 158
Beth's Story 171
Phil's Story 174
Doug's Story 180

Outcomes 188
Epilogue 189

Appendix of Curriculum Vitaes / Resumes
Grant 193
Ron 199
Rob 207
Chris 221
Paula 225
Beth 227
Phil 235
Doug 237

Introduction

This book is about a family of eight brothers and sisters who grew up in a middle-class Catholic neighborhood in Dayton, Ohio, around and after World War II. My first intention was to keep our family lore alive, but as my writing proceeded, I realized that I was describing a lot about Dayton in some of its greatest moments. Despite the recent Great Depression and a dangerous world war, the 1950s was a kinder time and a period of prosperity in Dayton. Dayton was a hotbed of inventions and factories, and many of its products were sold around the world.

I also realized that this book contains considerable commentary about the state of Catholic education at the time. Anyone interested in parochial schools will find strong testimony to the benefits of Catholic schools for our family. We matured in a culture that helped us make good choices and provided the freedom to flourish in the American Dream.

We were taught to be ethical and responsible at an early age, but we also had a lot of fun. We were fortunate to have two outstanding parents, who came from the so-called "Greatest Generation." Their love for family and children was remarkable.

In writing this book, I wanted you to live with us and understand us as we were. I have gathered stories from each of the eight of us. I love the different flavorings my siblings have added to their memories of common events, like

Christmas morning, family dinners, sibling relationships, and school events. In addition, I have provided ancestry and photographs from over the years.

Remember that all of us are too soon forgotten. I hope these stories will help us live with you a little longer.

And all eight of us agree that:

Eight is Great!

Mom & Dad on a cruise on the Great Lakes
early in their marriage

THE BOOK OF GRANT

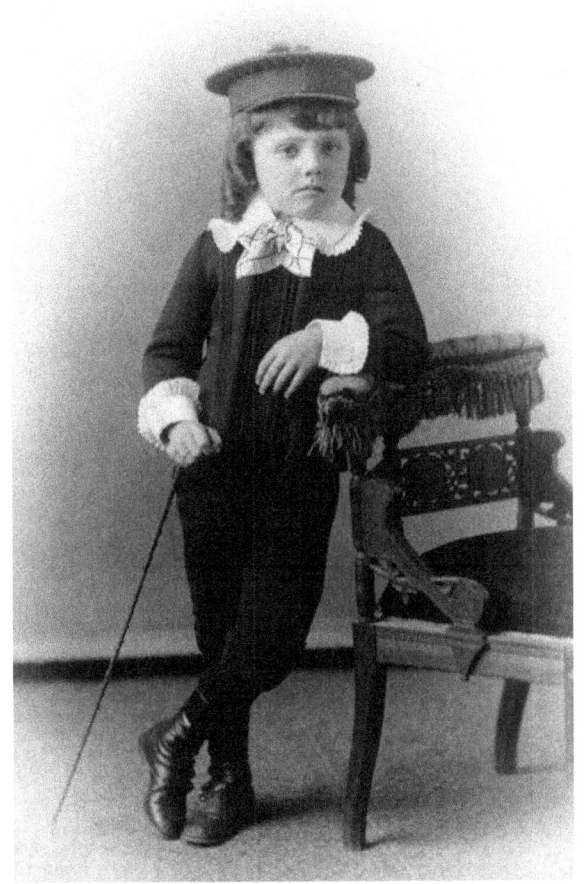

Photographs of the early 1900s era were often quite formalized. We think this is my grandfather Urban Deger.

Where The "Eight" Came From— Basic Genealogy

My paternal grandfather, Urban Deger, 1885 – 1962
Urban was born in Dayton, Ohio, on October 15, 1885. He was classically trained at the Cincinnati Conservatory of Music. He taught piano and organ and served as choir director for several Catholic Parishes in Dayton, Ohio. In those days there were three daily Masses (6 AM, 6:30 AM, and 7 AM) at our parish (Corpus Christi) requiring an organist to sing the responses. Urban claimed that he attended more Masses than Pope Pius XII. Grandfather played organ at the silent movies downtown, where music set the stage for the villain and the hero, danger, and serenity.

Grandfather Ubran's classic studio

With good intentions, Urban tried to teach me piano when I was nine or so. Typically, I was focused on friends, sports, and neighborhood adventures. Piano and grandpa lost out. I lost out. It was thirty years later when I appreciated my familial disposition for music. I took up piano in 1981, and for five years I could bring Mozart, Chopin, Bach, Beethoven, and Debussy alive at my fingertips.

By 2008, when I retired from medical practice, I joined two large choral groups as a tenor. Another word about Urban ... when he serenaded us at our family piano, he could always make us laugh by taking out his dentures and placing them atop the piano. Grandpa was a kind man appreciated by the family. He died of congestive heart failure on August 4, 1962 age 76 in Good Samaritan Hospital in Dayton.

From left: Elizabeth (Urban's mother), Dad, Uncle Tom, Agnes, Urban, an unidentified woman, and Urban's father John

My paternal grandmother, Agnes (Hochwalt) Deger, 1887 – 1974

Agnes, on the other hand, adopted more of the German stiffness and less of the beer-and-polka German culture. I don't remember her smiling or telling jokes. She was born April 8, 1887, and grew up in some luxury. Her father shared ownership of the Schwind Brewing Company in Dayton. As a young lady she was driven about in a Pierce Arrow automobile with a fringe on the top. Unfortunately, the brewery shut down during prohibition and never reopened. Much of the family fortune was lost. In her dotage Agnes was into hoarding hairnets, stockings, pins, and brooches. Her fox-skin stole was fun for us to investigate. It was constructed of two full independent fox skins. The mouths of the two foxes were spring-set so that the mouth of one fox could clamp on the tail of the other to form a ring about her neck to protect her from the weather. Agnes was always reluctant to invite her grandchildren into her home, presumably because she accurately assessed that we would create havoc and mess. In her dotage in a Catholic nursing home, she became paranoid and accused a nearby lady of stealing her Easter hat. She died of influenza on July 10, 1974, at age 87.

Coelestine Schwind and Thomas Hochwalt home overlooking Miami River, where our father Robert John Deger was born February 1913

Agnes and Urban were urban heroes in 1913 just two weeks after my Dad was born. The Great Miami River flooded downtown Dayton, leaving many homeless. Living on the high bank, Urban and Agnes took stranded people into their home until the floodwaters receded. Several years later the Urban Degers moved with my father and his older brother Tom to Dayton View on Wroe Avenue. After Dad and Uncle Tom were raised, my grandparents moved to Sunnyview Avenue.

My maternal grandfather, Joseph Grant, 1891 – 1951
Joseph was born August 25, 1891, in Springfield, Ohio, and worked for General Motors in the Oldsmobile Division in Michigan. At the time of this writing, I am not sure of his title. He was little known to us because he died July 17, 1951, age 59, of a myocardial infarction and smoking. We knew him to be a pleasant, nice man. My mother and her brother, Uncle Joe, and myself inherited the bad cholesterol gene from grandfather Grant. Uncle Joe, also a cigarette smoker, passed at 57 and mom had her first heart attack at age 65, somewhat young for a woman. I have been lucky so far because of effective anti-cholesterol medicines not available to my predecessors, and I was able to stop smoking by the age of 26.

The family Grant was of Scottish English descent. The town of Grantshire is located in the Scottish Highlands. The partially destroyed Uhrkarht Castle on the north shore of Loch Ness was once a holding of the Clan Grant. The Grant surname became my first name and I am proud of it. Yet in my imagination I suspect the tough McDonalds, or the Campbells, beat the crud out of the little Grants. Grandfather Joe's dad was a dentist in Springfield, Ohio, and made some purchases of land. I've seen some of the documents of the Grant plats in Springfield, Ohio.

The Seven Briggs Sisters: Grace Wilkin, Willa Ackert, Mazie Whitmore, Vera Grant (our grandmother), Nettie Kennedy, and (seated) Bessie Lafferty, Kate LeSuerer, Grandma Mary Josephine Briggs, and Charles Briggs Ackert

My maternal grandmother, Vera Winifred (Briggs) Grant, 1891 – 1969

Vera was our most favored grandparent. She was the one we spent the most time with, partially because of her relatively early widowhood. But she also possessed a lot of common sense, good character, and love of having fun. We affectionately called her "Nana." She was born March 9, 1891, on a farm south and east of Dayton in Chillicothe County. Her father's name was Rufus Briggs, a farmer in rural Ohio. Guess what color his hair was? This honorable man was allegedly out tilling the front 40, when the midwife called out the window to tell him that he had another red-haired daughter (our Vera). It is said that he just kept on plowing. Indeed, a total of 7 red-haired daughters were given to Rufus and his wife Mary. Their names were Grace, Willa, Vera, Nettie (Janet), Daisy, Maisy, Bessie, and Kate. We've visited the Chillicothe County Courthouse and found the records of the farm. We found one of the old gravesites and the newer consolidated cemetery. We also found the remains of the old red brick schoolhouse they attended.

Nana lived with us for a while after grandpa died. For some reason, that didn't sit well with Dad. He probably just needed some peace and solitude at that point in his life. Nana moved to a small apartment several blocks away on Fountain and Wheatley Avenues. Nana took time to enjoy card games with me. She taught me Canasta, a really engaging card game much like the current "Hand and Foot." Nana was a tease. "I wonder what's to be done with that full wastebasket?" she might say. The translation meant, "Grant, would you empty that wastebasket?" When her arthritis acted up, she would declare that she "had a bone in her leg" and would beckon me to bring her the sewing basket. In later years, Grandma Grant let me borrow her hot blue and white '53 Chevy. I was always grateful for her kindness, since my '47 Chevy was dishwater brown and shaped like an armadillo.

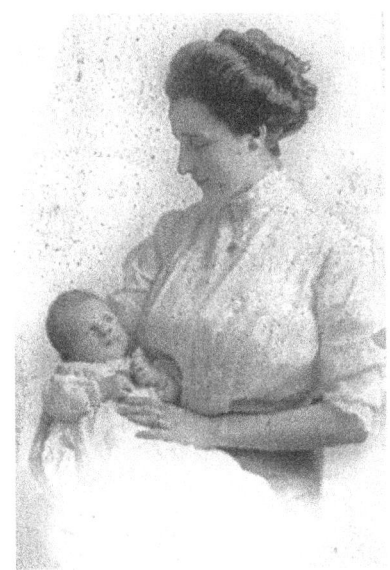

Grandmother Agnes Deger with her newborn son, Robert John, our father

Nana needed a source of income and found several jobs, usually in retail. But her best and most interesting work was serving as housemother to a sorority house at Wittenberg College, a fine Lutheran institution of learning in Springfield, Ohio. Proper decorum and behavior were expected of the young ladies, and Nana enforced the rules. Each evening there was a common dinner including proper place settings and the recitation of grace before partaking. Young males from nearby fraternities could earn a little money by serving the girls. Ten PM was the curfew on weekdays, and 11 or 12 PM on weekends. We siblings have recently visited the old sorority house, which remains intact and still functions as a sorority. A 1963 group picture of Nana with her young ladies adorns the main hall of the house to this day. Nana did set me up with a date or two. I would never have misbehaved for any number of reasons. I was seriously engrossed in medical studies, was not very worldly wise, and was restrained by Catholic guilt where there was a risk of potential concupiscence.

Nana died February 11, 1969, age 77. By that time, I was an impoverished medical resident at Mayo Clinic in Rochester, Minnesota, and did not attend her funeral. I should have. I loved her.

My father, Robert John Deger, 1913 – 1998
My father was born in that large red brick home overlooking the Great Miami River on February 23, 1913. Later, his parents moved my father and his older brother Tom to Wroe Avenue in the domain of Corpus Christi parish. Dad planted a tree in that backyard which I believe still survives to this day. Dad had a lifelong interest in biology and followed that trend into St. Louis Medical School, a Jesuit university. Dad was a family practitioner from 1936 until his retirement in 1988. He delivered 2,900 babies and made countless house calls. He was on the staff of Good Samaritan and St. Elizabeth hospitals. He

served as Medical Director of Maria Joseph Living Care Center and Mercy Sienna Woods Center.

Dad was quiet, reserved, tall 6 ft. 3 in. tall, and Lincolnesque, although handsome. In those days medicine was more a calling than a job, and Dad was very hard working. He

Uncle Tom Deger, Ruth Hanbush, Robert Deger (our Dad), and unknown - 1918

would rise early to shovel coal into the furnace on Salem Avenue. Oil heat at 617 Kenilworth must have made his life a little easier.

Seventy-hour work weeks were not rare. He would come home late, eat by himself (would you want to eat with 8 kids after a long day?), handwrite his records in his den, and go to bed. I've seen his records ... an office call in the late 1950s cost $3. A medical record for the entire family could be handled on a 4x7 card. The patriarch's name was listed first, then came the name of the family member being treated, the date, the diagnosis, and the charge. A small x noted that the charge had been paid. Most people paid in cash. Some poor people paid with tennis balls or fish they caught, or some temporary work, or often, nothing at all. Dad did a lot of pro bono work. His calling often kept him up at nights delivering a baby, setting a bone, or taking out a gallbladder. He had no bookkeeper or staff except for one office nurse. He had no Medicare to deal with, and malpractice attorneys were as scarce as a safe nuclear pact with Iran or North Korea.

Dad's major treats and weaknesses were to be found in his small office refrigerator. Hershey Bars and Coca-Colas in the old 6 oz. glass bottles were found next to the penicillin and insulin vials. Malted Milk Balls sat on the shelf next to the refrigerator. Dad was always trim and apparently undamaged by his choice of snacks.

Dad seemed to understand the limits of medical care in his day. He was known for his kindly bedside manner, but not for overprescribing or pushing for aggressive treatments. The only time he administered a penicillin shot to me, the old-fashioned glass syringe with a large bore needle jammed and the shot had to be redone. These big needles were sterilized after each use and sometimes re-sharpened. Today injection systems are disposed of after one use.

People would stop him anywhere to ask free advice, especially it seems after church. I recall patients asking him to look at their throats or tongues as our family was exiting the service. Another time Dad's car was beckoned over and stopped by a patient on busy Salem Avenue when he was in the process of driving us all to my medical school graduation in Cincinnati in 1965.

When Dad died age 85 on October 10th, 1998, of bladder cancer (a complication of a lifetime of cigarette smoking), people testified at the wake of his many kindnesses. "He delivered my baby for free when we had no money." Some of the kids he delivered are still friends of mine. Dad's favorite respite was a good game of tennis. Bob Meininger, one of Dad's favorite tennis partners, wanted to insert a can of tennis balls next to his body in the coffin, but for dignity's sake I would not permit that. In retrospect, I think it was a loving gesture.

Dad worked much too hard, but he did the best he could with his flock. He took the family to Indian Lake for a week of fishing and swimming. He occasionally played tennis with us. Together we tediously built a 16-foot wooden boat from a Chris Craft Kit in the basement. It had a thousand screws. The boat did not clear the basement door, however, until some framing was removed. But the *Wet Pet* served us well at Indian Lake for years. It had a 7.5 HP Evinrude engine, not enough to get us up on skis, but enough for fun, fishing, and swimming around the lake.

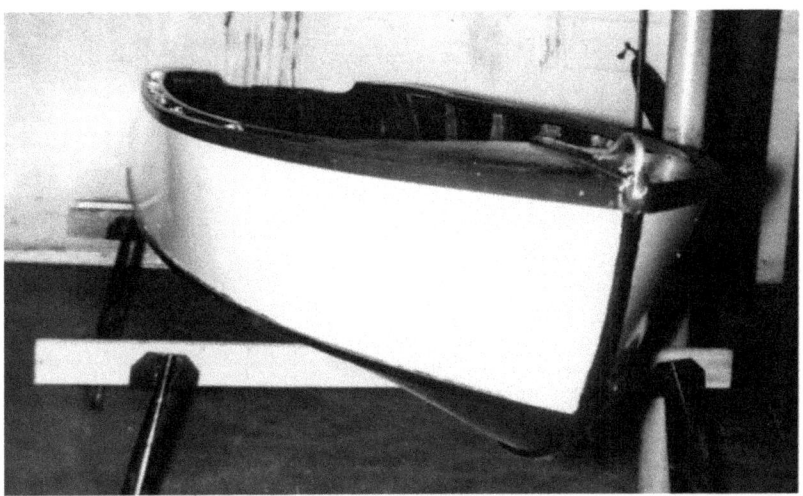

We built the "Wet Pet" in our basement and almost couldn't get it out - 1950s

Having two parents who themselves struggled to pay for an education and find work during the Great Depression unconsciously sent interesting messages to me. There were many pressures on my parents to provide for eight children. Money was very carefully dispersed. I felt in some ways that we were poor. The fact was however, that we never lacked food, shelter, tuition to Catholic Schools, or reasonable clothing. But we were clearly careful and cautious with money as a family. The good news for me is that I formulated useful lessons about saving and long-term economic goals that kept me in good stead.

My mother (Winifred Ann Grant), 1916 - 1992
My mother was born on August 16, 1916, in Royal Oaks, Michigan to Joseph and Vera Grant. Mom was the eldest of three children. Her brother Joe Jr., and her sister Phyllis completed their family. Uncle Joe lived in California. Once when he visited Dayton, we asked him if Californians still wore 6-shooters out there. Aunt Phyllis was a cheery woman who reminded me a lot of Nana. Aunt Phyllis married Don Maliskey, a career Army Officer who was stationed all over the world. Their children were born on three different continents. They retired in Huntsville, Alabama, where Don was working with folks

Mother - 1938

who created rocket development for the United States Military. Werner Von Braun, who created the V-2 rocket for Germany during WWII, was lured to Huntsville after the war.

There was some blue blood in Mother's background. Some Boston cousins (Sally Hews Phillips McClenahan was one) lived on historic Beacon Hill where 17th century windows would slowly turn blue because of their cobalt content. Mom's great uncle, ZeBarney Thorne Phillips, was once the Dean of the entire Episcopal Church in the United States. We have a picture of ZeBarney, then Chaplain for the U.S. Senate and Dean of the National Cathedral, with Franklin Delano Roosevelt. Of note, the Reverend ZeBarney began his clerical ministries in a small Greystone church named St. Mary's in the humble southeastern Ohio town of Hillsboro. His name

Starting second left: Eleanor Roosevelt, ZeBarney Phillips, a cleric, Winston Churchill, FDR and his doctor

can still be found on a plaque in that church. Dressed in black and giving recitations in Latin, he was no doubt an impressive figure who rose to the top of his calling.

Mother was a very gifted student who was allowed to bypass two high school years to attend college early. She graduated from Ypsilanti High School as Valedictorian at age 16, and wrote an invocation for her class in Latin. But those were the days of great economic collapse, so her college days in Lansing were numbered. Mom and her sister Phyllis migrated to the more entrepreneurial city of Dayton to seek employment. Mom found work in the office of a young physician by the name of Robert Deger and the rest is, well, our history.

Mother was a practicing Episcopalian when she met Dad, but soon became a Catholic. I tell you the Catholic Church was lucky to gain her. As so many converts do, she became a stalwart of the parish. She loved all the parish social and religious functions (St. Patrick's Day, Fish Fries, Catholic School PTA, Cub Scouts leadership, etc.). She was strongly pro-life, and a member of the Block Rosary group. Mom was intensely proud of her large family and was pleased to raise us in the best tenets of the Faith.

The way I see it is that in a different time and mindset, Mom could easily have held the keys to the Executive Bathroom. Instead, she claimed the hearts of her large family who all did well because of her loving guidance. She calmed many a tiff among siblings, mended many a cut or bump, and loved us when we were sad or scared. She loved me through the measles and the mumps (no vaccines in those days). She tolerated with forbearance the loss of treasured personal artifacts (small china cups and tiny horse figurines) to unauthorized footballs and roughhousing. Most of all, she had a clarity about kindly, ethical behavior which she gave us freely in word and deed.

She neither smoked nor drank. Once at Christmas dinner she had a small glass of Mogen-David wine (a cheap sweet variety bought at the nearby Jewish delicatessen) and her face glowed all day. There was nothing she enjoyed more than the 8 of us around the table telling stories about our growing up. She laughed heartily, even if she was the butt of some of our misdeeds. Mother almost always seemed optimistic and happy because she found good in most people and events.

As we became educated and married, she could hardly bear to see us depart. She always wept as we left. She was always anxious for our every word when we returned. When Mom was 65, she decided to take a college course at the University of Dayton. She got an "A" and never took another course, as if to say, "See, I can still do it!"

Mom's health risks included hypertension, hypercholesterolemia, and poor family history of early coronary artery disease. She suffered a heart attack at age 65 and died February 5, 1992, age 75, after several years of congestive heart failure. She passed suddenly of cardiac arrest at home while having breakfast with Dad.

May God give her perpetual peace and hold her in His hands. I hope she knows how much we loved her. She was our moral compass. She was our guide to making proper judgments, finding one's way in life, and serving others. She and Dad were married more than 53 years.

Look what our parents started: Grandmother Agnes, Dad, & Mom in front - 1972

A Touching Example of Mother's Thinking in Her Own Words
A tumultuous year ends happily with the birth of our brother Douglas, the eighth and last of the Deger siblings. Mom was 40 when she wrote "A Life Really Did Begin at Forty" for a writer's workshop in 1957.

Here is what Mother wrote:
When I hear the phrase "Life Begins at Forty", I recall my life at that age---and feel that God was guiding me and my family through a most unusual year. For a life did begin at forty!

A few weeks after my birthday, our local newspaper called and asked to do a feature story on a big family at the start of the school year. So, they came, took pictures, wrote up our daily routines—describing my round-the-clock busy general practitioner husband, who had a heavy office practice, made house calls, took phone calls day and night. They detailed my day taking care of nine-month Philip, managing a house with six active grade and high school children. I smile as I recall the poses taken for the article---the three big boys ages eighteen, sixteen, fourteen, combing their hair and adjusting their ties in front of one-bathroom mirror; me with baby Phil on my lap, combing six-year-old Beth's hair, while Paula, eight, and Christine, eleven, look on. That wasn't at all true to real life, but it was fun to be "Written Up!"

School did start, and I did my usual housework, plus carrying baskets of peaches home from the fruit farm to make into pies for the freezer; carrying groceries and three-gallon cartons of ice cream for the freezer---(In fact my neighbor and I were so enthusiastic about going to the Gem City Ice Cream plant and stocking up, that my family now politely refuse such goodies.)

I first noticed back pain that Fall while climbing steps to watch a football game in the University of Dayton stadium. I also remember pushing Baby Phil in a stroller over at Kettering Field to watch son Bob play eighth-grade football and finding it difficult to climb up the slope to our car, because of the severe pain. It became so excruciating that we finally made an appointment to see a neurosurgeon in his office. But before we could keep the date, I was in such agony that the doctor sent me into the hospital. After a myelogram and other tests, when he told me on a Monday morning that he and his partner would operate on Wednesday, I was relieved, and thought "Why wait? Why not now?"

I also remember a friend of mine saying "Well, Winnie, at least you're not pregnant". To which I replied----"Oh, but I am!" So, two months pregnant, I underwent a laminectomy (a slipped disc operation). I did very well—within a week up walking in the hall ready to go home, when I developed phlebitis, and had to stay in the hospital another two-and a half weeks. These were sober times--a baby nearing his first birthday, Christmas coming, a big family needing me. I reached a stage of mild depression toward the end of my stay, and will never cease to be grateful to a nurse who came in my room to give me a back rub, smooth the sheets, utter words of encouragement. Gratefully, I did go home to a different kind of holiday, where I had to let others lift my baby son and do for me. Thank God for loving family and kind friends!

Meanwhile, in March, we had another short article and picture in the University of Dayton Alumni magazine. This time Big Brother Grant was playing the piano, with little Phil sitting on his lap. The rest of us are grouped around the piano—and a very sober Mama looks somberly into the camera!

To add to all the complications of this year, we had decided to purchase the home of a neighbor in the next block, who was building a new house, to be finished in April. While I was hospitalized, my husband showed our home to just one couple, who promised to buy it at our price, pay cash, and wait until April to move in. So, on a rainy, cold Good Friday morning, we moved into our spacious, lovely old brick home, which was to be our haven for eighteen years.

The move proved to be a bit too much for me, however. At my next OB appointment, the doctor took one look at my swollen face and body, squinty eyes, yellowish complexion, and ordered me into the hospital. I remember getting off the bus, stopping in my friend's house to tell her that I had to go in that afternoon, and wondering how I would ever be able to arrange it. But in I went, to spend a week of rest, extensive medication to clear up the toxemia. On April 30, the doctor induced labor. Because of my poor condition, and a seven-and a half month pregnancy, a nurse later confided to me that they didn't really expect the baby to live. But to our great joy, Douglas, at four pounds, five ounces, was normal and healthy. Our oldest son Grant was working in the lab at Good Samaritan Hospital, and took me in a wheel chair to the "Preemie" nursery for my first glimpse of this miracle baby. His weight dropped to three pounds, fifteen ounces at a week, but our pediatrician assured us that he was fine, so we left him in the nursery for ten more days.

I had been concerned all spring about being able to attend our Grant's high school, and Bobby's eighth-grade graduations in June, since Doug's original due date was June 17. But once again, the Good Lord smoothed the path for us by his early arrival. So, we were able to attend both occasions. On the morning of Bob's ceremonies, Doug shot a fever and an earache. Our kind pediatrician, Dr. Jones, who lived across the street, obligingly came to give a shot of penicillin, and assure me he would be O.K. to leave.

Being so tiny, Doug had to be fed every three hours, and at the age of two months weighed only eight pounds. But I feel that God helped and guided us through this whole traumatic experience. In spite of my major surgery, a great deal of medications, x-rays (considered so dangerous to a fetus), that little fellow continued to thrive. He's always had the best disposition in the world, been a best friend to Phil, fun for all his family to be around. He has grown into a confident, extroverted, cheerful adult----a computer salesman, no less!

A life _did_ begin at forty----and he's THE JOY OF MY OLD AGE!

Mom survived raising eight children and could still smile

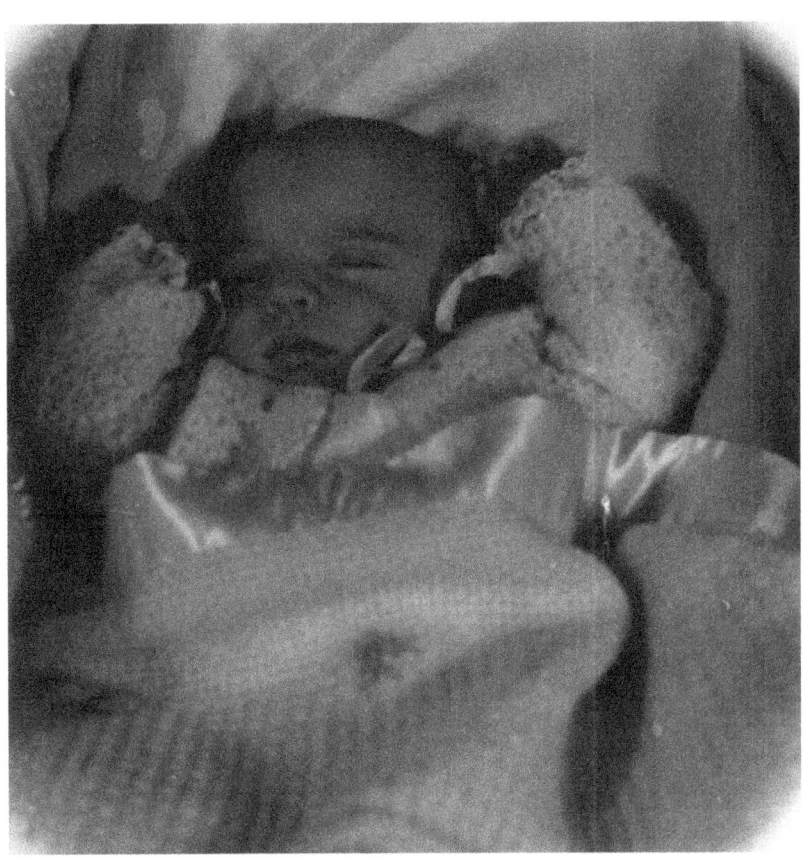

Grant Edward Deger – 7 weeks old – November 1939

In the Beginning

One's earliest factual memories are difficult to separate from hazy recollections of old photographs or family tales. For example, I do not remember being in a bathtub with Carol Ann Foy when we both were somewhat short of two years of age, but there is a photograph to prove it. The bath probably was fun, suds and all. Dr. Foy (Carol Ann's father) was my father's best friend. There were great hopes for their respective first children. But naked in a tub together at age 20 months? Give me a break. For the record, we never bathed together again. Having been such a nerd around women all my life, I have carefully secured that photo. You may have a copy for a minimal fee.

My baby book was huge, the largest no doubt of all the eight Deger children, because maternal energy is inversely proportional to the number of new babies. I had the benefit of an energetic mother collecting measurements, pictures, invitations, names of friends, and all sorts of memories for her first born. I have raided that book for photos and data for this book.

What seems to be my first independent memories are those of being at my mother's knee with my brother Ron, as she read Dad's letters to us. It was war time. Dad had been called to serve in the Army Air Corps (the United States Air Force had not yet been invented). Dad was stationed at Bradley Air Base, Windsor Locks, Connecticut, just north of

Hartford. He was sent to the Army Base to treat patients, some of whom were German prisoners-of-war. By the way, I think it is funny that my dad, an Army Air Corps Captain, was terrified of airplanes and never flew (except once in 1968 when he accompanied his dying best friend Dr. Foy to the Mayo Clinic in Rochester, Minnesota.) Sadly, Dr. Foy's brain tumor was untreatable.

Windsor Locks, Connecticut - 1945

Mother was pregnant with brother Bobby while waiting to be called from Dayton to join Dad at Bradley Air Base. We missed our father, and his letters kept him symbolically with us. He would adorn his writings with hand-drawn cartoon characters from the 1940s newspapers. And Dad was a pretty good drawer too. You may be too young to remember Li'l Abner, The Katzenjammer Kids, Henry, Mary Worth, Little Lulu, the Little King, or Dick Tracy, but for most of America these were the prime cartoon treats in WWII era Sunday newspapers.

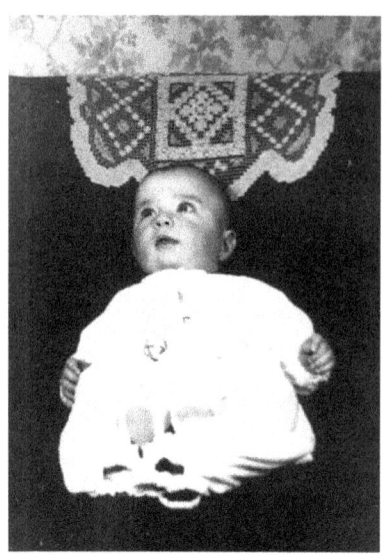
Grant at 4 months

But I digress. I got too far ahead. I need to tell you that Grant Edward was born at St. Elizabeth Hospital at 2:58 PM on Friday, September 15, 1939. Dr. Norman Hochwalt, a relative of my grandmother's, was the obstetrician. I weighed in at 5 lbs. 13 oz., and have been behind the height curve most of my life. At the time of this writing I am 79 years old, 5 ft. 8 in. tall, and a beefy 183 lbs., about 25 lbs. beyond my college weight. But I exercise regularly, so I suspect much of the beef has a muscular component. I frequently say that my goal for 2018 is a 10-pound weight loss, and I've only got 15 to go.

I don't know if my birth created any excitement, but I do know that Hitler invaded Belgium shortly thereafter. My parents seemed anxious to get a family started and took a chance on me. I arrived 10 months and two weeks after their wedding in Alma, Michigan, on November 5, 1938. The doctor apologetically told my parents that he did the best he could, but I survived anyhow. (Plagiarized from Rodney Dangerfield.)

Our First Home

The nascent Deger family lived at 1325 Salem Avenue in North Dayton View. Dad had purchased a two-story home on the corner of Salem and Fountain Avenues. It came with a generous yard front and back, some large trees and shrubs. I recall a huge patch of lilies on the northeast side of the house. In the back there was a shallow cement wading pool about 10 feet across. My parents felt it posed a risk for toddlers and quickly filled in the pond with sand, which was just as much fun. A fence now separates the old house from two large apartment buildings on the south side, which were built several years after we arrived. So initially there were some extra forested lots to play in. The upstairs was family space. The main floor was Dad's medical office. His patients entered by the front entrance on Salem Avenue. His wife and offspring walked past the old coal cellar doors to the back porch and up the back stairway. A garage and driveway formed the eastern exposure, facing north to Fountain Avenue. Salem Avenue, otherwise known as State Route 49, was a busy thoroughfare, two lanes in each direction stretching from Goshen north of Cincinnati, across the Miami River to the Salem address where Dad was born, on to North Dayton where we lived as a family, onward to Trotwood (where we could purchase fireworks), and then dissipating somewhere in the middle of western Ohio near Indian Lake.

In those times, horse-drawn vans would bring fresh milk and bakery goods, and sometimes fruits and vegetables, into the neighborhoods. Milk was not yet homogenized. In the winter milk would freeze in the glass quart bottles on the back porch. Water expands when frozen, so the paper milk cap would rise, exposing an inch of frozen cream above the mouth of the glass bottle. Margarine was introduced as a butter substitute. It was basically a white mushy fat. Initially, the butter industry would not allow the margarine to be colored to look like butter. So, margarine came in a soft plastic pack with a pellet of yellow coloring inside the plastic wrap. One would squash the pellet and repeatedly squish the white fat and the coloring together for five minutes. And lo, a butter-like product appeared, looking a bit more appealing than white fat. My brother Ron and I would often toss the margarine packet around like a football. And only once do I remember the packet breaking open.

Grant & Ron taken in Windsor Locks, Connecticut - 1942

My first brother Ronald Thomas came along on May 21, 1941. He was a cheerful child and we had lots of fun, especially physical fun, like bear cubs. Unfortunately, accidents do happen. Once I pushed him and he tumbled onto a tree root in the backyard and broke a collar bone. He was two years younger, but after a few more years he grew larger than me. The vigor of our bear-cub-like combat increased somewhat over time. When the next Deger brother, Robert Jr., matured, he could join with me in a coalition against Ron. However, allegiances do shift and sometimes Ron and I beat up on Rob just for fun. I will mention the notorious caper of the peach tree later. But when the chips were down, we fiercely defended each other from external harm. Brucie Haynes comes to mind, a ferocious little neighborhood kid who would throw golf-ball-sized rocks at you and started a gang in his teen years. Otherwise, we three male siblings made instant playmates inside or outdoors, often on trees and bikes. We loved family touch football, backyard basketball, and sports of all kinds.

Grant, Ron, & Bobby on the grounds of
Dayton's beautiful Art Institute - 1946

Grant & Ron on the fender of one of Dad's 26 successive Fords - 1942

World War II

My second brother, Robert John, was born June 7, 1943, at Good Samaritan Hospital in Dayton. Very shortly (weeks) after Bobby's birth, we were called to join Dad in Windsor Locks, Connecticut, at the Army Air base. Unfortunately, Rob contracted whooping cough as we were leaving. Can you imagine our poor mother on a cross-country train trip nursing a new baby with a potentially lethal respiratory infection while tending to two other very young children?

In time, Robert Jr. rejected his childhood name of Bobby and made us call him Rob, which took me some time to assimilate. The reason, I think, is that as the first four kids came along, it was harmonic to say we were, "Grant, Ronnie, Bobby, and Chrissy." My name Grant was incorruptible. No one ever created a nickname that stuck, except that Dad called me "Little Doc" in my infancy. It was prophetic. I never had a chance to become anything other than a doctor.

Life at Windsor Locks was fun. Mom and Dad rented the upstairs of a semi-rural two-story farmhouse. There were spacious grounds, with a chicken coop, large gardens, fruit trees, a swing set, and woods. We had lots of room to enjoy being young boys. The landlord had cats that we chased. I lived there for two years starting at age 4.

This white house sat high above the street. A tall cement wall supported the downward sweeping front lawn and abutted the sidewalk below. I recall the sidewalk well, because Ron and I decided to take out on our own and got several blocks away. Imagine mother's horror to lose her little boys. Finally, a neighbor in his car made some circles around the neighborhood and brought us home, blissfully unaware that we had done wrong (until mothers' sorrow and admonitions brought us back to reality).

Grant, Ron, Rob - Windsor Locks, Connecticut - 1944

The house did overlook the Locks of Windsor. I vividly remember the smoke and flames of a plane crash into the water of the locks in front of our house. An American pilot lost his life when his two-engine propeller plane hit some wires and crashed into the water. By the way we saved tin cans and lard for the war effort. Mom seriously cut her thumb while crushing a tin can and had to be taken by Dad to the Base emergency room. As requested by the War Department, Dad painted the top half of his Ford's headlights with black paint, so the car would be less visible to enemy planes and submarines. There were periodic warning sirens and safety exercises during the Great War, even in Connecticut. But we were safe and happy and too young to appreciate the drama and danger of international war.

Grant, Ron, and cousin Kim Maliskey in Windsor Locks, Connecticut 1943

The grounds of our home there did have a swing set as I mentioned. Brother Bobby, a mere infant, walked in front of a moving occupied swing and sustained a forehead laceration, the scar of which is slightly visible to this day some 73 years later. I remember attending the Air Base Thanksgiving Dinner with my family. My voluminous baby-book still has a formal menu printed for that holiday dinner. I remember trying to throw a basketball toward the hoop at the Base gym.

Many, many years later I took a trip to visit my son Matthew, an aerospace engineer working for Pratt-Whitney Co. in Hartford, Connecticut. I wagered the hope that the old Windsor Locks home could still be found. By golly, we not only found the home on the main street of Windsor above the Locks, but it remained almost exactly as I had remembered it. The lock's gates, which raised and lowered the slowly flowing water, were still there. The tall cement wall holding the front yard back from the sidewalk was still there. The house was still there; white, undivided, and sitting on several acres. It kept its rural feeling in a small city. We rang the doorbell and met with the current owner, who was amused and pleased that someone who lived there over 60 years earlier was returning for a visit.

My first sister and the fourth of the Deger Clan, Christine Louise, was born in Connecticut on August 1, 1945. She would have no memories of Windsor Locks, as we were about to return to Dayton, Ohio, in the autumn of 1945. There my Dad would resume his medical practice and we would live again in the upstairs of his office at 1325 Salem Avenue. I remember my parents making plans to return, and that our Dayton home would require renovations to hold us all. So, I was to live with my Uncle Paul and Aunt Dorothy Agnew for several months in the interim. I enjoyed my time with cousins Phyllis, Dorothy, and Tom Agnew, who would walk with me to school that Fall season. Aunt Dorothy (Grandmother Agnes Deger's sister) had some odd ideas. She insisted that one must have daily bowel movements, and attest they had done their physiologic duty. She also owned an alleged weight reduction machine. I say alleged because it was a 4-foot or so standing device with a wide strap that wrapped around your trunk and shook you furiously. I don't know why shaking would cause significant weight loss. Perhaps it contributed to bowel function.

As an aside, the Agnews sponsored a wonderful annual family Easter egg hunt for the Clan. Once we found a colored egg in a tree branch overlooked from the previous years' search. The Agnew home was on Stoddard Avenue, a serene area with large stone homes and generous well-landscaped lots. Their home was not far from the iconic Greek Orthodox Church and the classic Dayton Art Institute, both of which still stand elegantly above the Miami River in Dayton View. Uncle Paul was an engineer who died young of lung cancer from smoking.

At 1325 Salem Avenue again, Ronnie, Bobby, Chrissy, and "Little Doc" played in the backyard sandpit and tricycled down the sidewalks of Fountain Avenue. I remember dreaming for years of owning a real two-wheel bicycle, but none ever showed up in my Christmas or birthday stockings. It took real action and a deal with my father to gain that bicycle. I agreed to put up $13 of my own (I was an avaricious saver), and dad would pay the remaining $13 for the bike if I painted the entire backyard picket fence. I did, or nearly did the job, and the bike was mine. Among other work, I remember making some money shoveling snow for neighbors.

Corpus Christi Grade School

I remember arriving for the first grade at Corpus Christi Catholic School several weeks late because of our move from Windsor Locks. I was made to share a desk and seat with a distant cousin (David Deger), a large child twice my size. The sardine issue was soon resolved, however, and my career at Corpus Christi began. My father had also attended good old Corpus Christi (Latin for Body of Christ). Grandfather Urban Deger was choirmaster and organist there as well.

Corpus Christi holds some of the great memories of my life. There I met lifelong pals like Walt Reiling, John Jauch, Mike Barlow, Jim Brogan, Vic King, Lee Buddendeck, Herb

Clemens, Howard Herolzer, Bill Pflaum, Tom Miller, George Beemsterboer, Bob Homewood, and many others. These were real and decent buddies who shared the fullness of baseball, basketball (in alleys, yards, gyms, and side-lots), laugh-ins, sleep-ins, bicycling, Cub Scouts, church bingo, hot chocolate and donuts on First Fridays in the school basement,

First Holy Communion - 1946

St. Patrick's Day parties, and service as altar boys and choir boys. Later, the same guys shared high school, double dates, Boy Scouts, newspaper routes, soda jerking, dance hops, proms, etc. More on the high school days later. I even went to college with some of these guys. I even attended medical school with other friends from the parochial school system in Dayton.

At Corpus Christi grade school, the good Sisters of Charity nudged us along to basically good lives with good ethics, patriotism, and solid educational foundations. The Vatican recently canonized the founder of the Order of the Sisters of Charity, St. Elizabeth Ann Seton.

Nothing was more beautiful in my childhood memories than our First Holy Communion. Here are the innocent pure young ones: boys in jackets, white shirts, ties, and pressed short pants; girls in white dresses with veils and white shoes and white socks. The Communicants-To-Be processed from the school to the church with up-lifted hands in the prayer position. It was a big deal with much anticipation and preparation. On a Sunday late in spring, our parents, grandparents, and sometimes godparents shared in this big event. They often gave small gifts such as prayer books, holy medals, and rosaries. A big family dinner followed.

Merry Christmas from Grant, Ronnie, Bobbie, Chrissy, Paula, and Bethie - 1951

Christmas Mass at Corpus Christi Church always holds special memories and warm feelings. Typically, we would attend the 6 AM service as a family. Snow was sometimes softly falling in the predawn glow of a really exciting day. The Mass was a High Mass, co-celebrated by three priests, and included blessing the congregation with incense, and chanting from the altar with responses by the choir. Grandfather Deger led the hymns before and during Mass from his place at the organ. He chose sweet and brilliant music that brought to mind the simple message of Christmas, the birth of Jesus. One piece he played every year was about the shepherds, the strains of which still warm my heart. I sang with the soprano boys, while the men sang the bass and tenor parts. To this day, a beautiful Christmas Mass means more to me than all the chaos of tearing open presents and overeating.

I believe we often walked the mile to grade school each way. If we needed to take the bus downtown, it cost 3 cents to ride and a penny to transfer to the ancillary bus. Mom gave me a nickel and expected the left-over penny to be returned. She was upset if I forgot and threw the entire nickel in the coin box at the bus driver's side. I am so glad my parents were young adults during the Great Depression. They taught us how to be frugal and productive and yet generous to those in need.

At Corpus Christi, we gathered in the school play yard until the school bell rang promptly at 8:30 AM. Mr. Schlosser, the school janitor, would often be wheelbarrowing the coal ashes from the school furnace to a dumping space across Orchard Avenue. Mr. Schlosser's daughter Martha, tall and lanky, started first grade with me, but was held back a grade for poor grades. We marched into our classrooms to the sound of a John Phillip Sousa march broadcast from the principal's office. Our first classroom duty was the recitation of the Pledge of Allegiance to the United States of America. Then followed a prayer that started the learning of the day. In mid-morning we enjoyed a 15-

Second grade picture of Grant

minute recess in the schoolyard. The upper-grade boys could play on the Five Oaks Park hill. A nutritious lunch was provided in the cafeteria, mostly by volunteer mothers. We stayed in the same classroom all day with the same teacher. Our church parish subsidized most of the tuition costs, and the dear nuns taught us without pay or union rules. Dad paid only a small fee and with eight kids, that was fortunate.

My first-grade teacher 72 years ago was Sister Modesta, a kind, quite elderly, nun who probably wasn't five feet in height. She dribbled a bit of saliva when she spoke. Sister Dolores Marie captained the ship in the second grade. My memory runs short here, but she was tall and ran a good ship. Miss Ann Landers taught the other third grade. Miss Landers was a no-nonsense lay person (not a nun). In her later years, however, she did enter the convent. I do not remember my third-grade teacher. There were two classrooms for every grade, and probably 30 kids in each classroom. Thus, there were likely over 400 kids enrolled in Corpus Christi.

Sister Mary Francis was the fourth-grade teacher. She taught the prospective altar boys the necessary Latin responses and the proper ways to assist the priest at Mass. During one after-school session, Sister was on the altar teaching prospective altar boys when to move the Mass Book from the Epistle side to the Gospel side. From somewhere in the dark quiet nave of the church, Mike Barlow passed seriously loud intestinal gas. Young boys just don't know how to restrain their laughter. Years later, Jim Brogan was assisting Monsignor Ansbury before Mass when he threw away a safety pin on the maniple (a cloth piece covering the priest's right arm), thinking it was left over from recent dry cleaning. Unfortunately, the pin was essential for securing the maniple to the priest's alb. And so, during Mass Father

Ansbury rapidly extended his arms proclaiming the Latin prayer "Dominus Vobiscum" (the Lord be with you). The maniple shot off into space, causing my guardian angel and me to snicker. Jim became a prominent respected lawyer (once a candidate for the Ohio State Supreme Court), yet often seemed a lovable absent-minded-professor. In later years Jim forgot coats and briefcases in restaurants, and even the name of his date.

Fifth grade must have been the "Amen Corner" of Corpus Christi Grade School. If you could survive the school's biggest and toughest nuns, you could make it in life. Sister Anna Marie and Sister Mary Raymond were large and stern and free with the ruler to the back of the hand. I believe it was Sister Anna Marie who bonked Norman Gunn's head into his desk for failing to pay attention. And I believe a paddle to one's backside in the cloakroom was used (very rarely) for the worst offenses. Our parents fully backed the Sister's discipline and often added some of their own. Contrast that classroom behavior with that of today's pupil-thugs who assault their teachers. Then their single-parent mother will often assault the teacher again. No wonder today's pupils fail to learn. We were the fortunate ones to have structure and guidance.

Miss Madonna Walk was a young and pretty newly hired lay teacher at a time when sixth- grade boys were beginning to discover gender differences. Our friend Jim Brogan was called to the blackboard to create a sentence and diagram its components: subject, verb, object, adverb, adjective, preposition, etc. He blurted out a sentence that embarrassed him and probably reflected his subconscious thinking. He wrote in chalk on the blackboard, "See Madonna walk." It was an easy sentence to diagram, but a hard one to live down when we were all laughing.

For those unaware of how the nuns chose their new names after taking vows, note that they took their parents' first names. Thus, our seventh-grade teacher, Sister Mary Thomas, had a mother named Mary and a father named Thomas. Sister Mary "Pear-Shape," as we nicknamed her, ran a serious seventh-grade classroom. She sentenced me to writing out the Constitution of the United States and inserting the part of speech over every word as punishment for throwing snowballs at the girls. One of Sister Mary Thomas's goals was teaching us to speak and debate. Fred Faust was booed for trying to convince us (out of his own ignorance) that cashews were made in factories from baked dough. Bill Pflaum won the debating contest because he was the only one who understood his declared topic.

First Fridays came once a month commemorating the crucifixion of Christ on Good Friday. Those days were a treat because after early Mass we were treated to hot chocolate and donuts in the school cafeteria. Walt Reiling had a mouthful of the chocolate-donut mixture when someone lit up his laughing center. The full contents of his mouth exploded across the table, splattering on the clothes of John Jauch and Bob Homewood.

Walt had another historic laughing spell at a most inappropriate time and place. He and I were serving Mass. Fr. Doyle had a big hole in the back of his sock. Prior to the changes of Vatican II, the priest said Mass facing the crucifix on the back wall rather than facing the congregation as is done today. As altar boys in white surplices and black cassocks, we knelt at the bottom of the altar peering directly at Fr. Doyle's socks. It makes no difference who first broke out in laughter, but Walt had a hearty laugh. And his laughter was always infectious. Sure enough, we simply could not cease until

Father briskly admonished us to stop snickering or leave the altar.

I just thought of another Walt episode. Picture this. We are kneeling in a neighbor's home with nearby neighbors and family saying the Rosary...the so-called "Block Rosary," which was popular then. It was great to socialize before and after, but the 20-minute rosary prayer was serious business. As I pulled my rosary from my pocket, it was obvious how tangled it was in rubber bands and string. The image of me straining to untangle my rosary was too much for Walt, who burst into snickering, which of course affected me. Our symbiotic chuckling was suppressed by stern advice to leave the room.

By the way, I need to tell you about an incident with Monsignor Ansbury and my grandfather Urban. Again, I was serving as altar boy. The Mass was in Latin, of course. "Dominus vobiscum" ("The Lord be with you") chanted our good monsignor. Grandfather Urban was a conscientious kapellmeister to be sure, but at this particular early morning Mass he must have been spaced out at the church organ. He was supposed to respond in chant, "Et cum Spiritu tuo" ("and with your Spirit"). Hearing no response, Fr. Ansbury repeated his cue, "Dominus vobiscum." Again, there was an embarrassing silence. Monsignor was so upset that he reflexively yelled out, "Can't you sing?" Faith-filled old ladies in the first two rows nearly fainted before grandfather finally responded.

Sister Francis Marie helped us through civics, math, English, history and the other usual eighth-grade subjects. We elected officers to run our Civics Club, sort of a student's forum helping us transform into adult life. Once our meeting was interrupted by an obviously upset Monsignor Ansbury. He rushed onto stage really peeved. Some of the boys on the playground on the hill had taken Bob McBride's pants and were throwing them up a tree. Monsignor noted that this was a

Graduating Class Corpus Christi Grade School, 1953. Monsignor Ansbury front & center

scandal beyond belief, especially since some non-Catholic neighbors witnessed the fracas. Monsignor spit fire as he impressed us that we would NEVER repeat such dastardly behavior. We could almost feel the Gates of Hell opening upon us.

Every year the eighth grade presented a class play. The class of 1953 based our drama (very loosely) on the opera Carmen. Jim Brogan and I were tasked to open a scene by carrying a long sign that read, "Day Breaks." And it really was funny when the sign broke in half at mid-stage. I'll never get my name in Broadway lights.

Sister Francis Beatrice was school principal long enough to know the Deger siblings as each of us climbed the grade ladder for eight years. Rob was sent to her office by his home class teacher to receive an award. But instead, the principal gave him a tongue lashing. Rob struggled to understand and asked why he was being punished instead of getting an award. Allegedly she stated, "Well, you are a Deger, aren't you?" I cannot vouch for the veracity of this story, but I do know that Rob had two active older brothers, the eldest of whom barely passed conduct (deportment). Indeed, Rob, who eventually had a history PhD, suffered downturns at Corpus Christi. In his second-grade, Sr. Evangelista was testing the students for their singing ability. She took Rob aside and said he "Sang like a crow." Maybe that's why he turned out to be a liberal.

Grades were reported on a two-leafed white sheet of paper. An "A" grade was 93% and above, a "B" grade was 85-92, and so on. Conduct was reported at the bottom of the sheet. I was generally in the "D" level there. Parents were required to sign the document demonstrating awareness of their child's abilities and weaknesses. It seems that I saved my intellectual and behavioral growth for high school when I developed a joy for learning. "A"s and good behavior came more easily after grade school.

I haven't said much about the girls in our classes, probably because we didn't spend time interacting with the opposite sex. We threw snowballs at them, and by the seventh grade noticed they were growing up. By the eighth grade, several of my male friends and I joined several of our classmates (Bobbie Klostermann, Dorothy Jacobs, Carole Maloney, and maybe Susan Hook), in once-a-month social evenings rotating at our parent's homes. We usually had snacks and pop, talked, and were home by 9:30 PM. I remember roller skating with a neighborhood girl once.

Our second home: 617 Kenilworth Avenue - 1948

Our Second Home

By 1948 it was clear that our expanding family needed more room. My second sister and fourth sibling, Paula Ann, was born August 1, 1948. That year we took up residence at 617 Kenilworth Avenue, a bit closer to church and school, and certainly lighter in traffic than busy Salem Avenue. Moreover, there were literally dozens of kids in all directions and most of them attended Corpus Christi School. Our home at 617 afforded us two stories to live in and a functional basement for our model Lionel train or building our boat, the *Wet Pet*. We had a dog named Duchess, found by Bobby and cared for by him. Then there was this weird parakeet named Nicki. Nicki had unusual privileges. The bird was allowed to fly freely in the house from time to time. By and by, the bird was quarantined for chewing the gilded edges of the living room mirror, and strewing droppings indiscriminately. Its tenure with us ended abruptly because of its freedoms. One brisk day I was leaving by the back door with a leather jacket on. Nicki landed on my right shoulder and I walked out the back door before fully realizing the bird's presence. Our dear pet was free! We called for Nicki the rest of the day, but she had no wish to live with a house full of crazy kids.

Bobbie and his enforcers Chrissy, Paula, & Bethie, run a neighborhood lemonade extortion business

Our backyard was not large, but had a peach tree, a basketball hoop, and a garage for Dad's succession of Ford automobiles. Over the years Dad purchased 26 Fords. When dad passed, Ford stock took a major tumble. An elderly couple, the Eberhardts, had the misfortune of living next door to our growing boisterous family. After millions of invasions by kids, balls (foot- base- and basket-), Easter chicks, bicycles, captive garter snakes, and water balloons, the Eberhardts erected a 6-foot chain fence between our backyards, which nicely kept the peace and their sanity. The Kaufmanns on the other side were protected from us by a wall along the driveway.

The personal needs of two parents and six kids were served upstairs by one toilet, sink, and tub, and downstairs with an additional sink and toilet. Can you imagine the competition for our sparse facilities? I often rose at 5 AM to finish my homework in peace and away from spilt milk. In fact, Vic King once sat in a chair full of spilt milk and thereafter would never sit down at our table until he checked the seats. The Dayton Daily News once featured pictures of our family preparing for a typical school day. These pictures included me tying my tie (required at Chaminade Catholic all-male high school), and others of us brushing teeth and vying for room about the mirror and sink.

Seven siblings start their day - September 1956

Our neighborhood was close to 70% Catholic then. It is no mystery why the neighborhood was connected to our parish. Within several blocks in each direction were large families of practicing papists. The Klostermanns across the street raised nine kids, the Dahms up the street nine as well. The families of Dineen, Neff, Smith, Wourms, Zits, Reiling, Herolzer, Heldorfer, Lipp, McBride, Cook, Smeltzer, Kellam, Danis, Boesch and Zimmer, added generously to the Catholic population of our fecund neighborhood. The minority Protestant kids who walked to Van Cleve public school a block from Corpus Christi were our friends, yet sort of considered unfortunate not to have what we had. I mean what's life without a parochial school, Sisters of Charity, bingo or St. Patrick's Day parties?

I just don't remember divorces, spousal abuse, burglaries, welfare abuse, or drugs. Our community was simply a nice middle-class neighborhood during some of America's finest hours. Dads with high school diplomas could raise large families and send their kids to colleges they themselves could not afford. It didn't take a PhD to develop some great businesses, and the political milieu was such that government didn't interfere. John Jauch's father shared in the ownership and management of Dayton Fabricated Steel and Dayton Stencil works. Mr. Jauch had an eighth-grade education and lots of common sense. Herb Clemens' dad (also an eighth-grade grad) ran his own plumbing company. Herb went on to become an internationally recognized PhD mathematician. Bill Pflaum's dad built a publishing company specializing in Catholic periodicals. The Pflaum Publishing Company's *Little Messenger* was read weekly around the United States in Catholic schools, including Corpus Christi. Walt Reiling's dad was a renowned Dayton surgeon and a great speaker. He was president of Optimists International, a service organization like Rotary. Mr. Dahm ran his own roofing company. Mr. Klostermann worked at National Cash Register Company, which literally built cash registers for the entire civilized world. These were our neighbors. Good people!

One of our Van Cleve public school friends was little Dick Braun, who suffered so from asthma. He wanted to be part of the action but died of obstructive lung disease as a young adult. Maybe he had cystic fibrosis. I don't know.

One of our non-friends was the previously mentioned neighborhood menace, Brucie Haynes. He was the first "American Sniper" with rocks. Years later in self-defense, Rob shot a Brucie associate named Jimmy Rupp in the leg with a B-B gun. Jimmy and Brucie had stolen Rob's new toy bow and arrow from him. Rob went home and got my B-B gun and told the boys to return his property, which they did. But Jimmy attacked, and Rob shot him in the leg. Brucie went on to associate with a small gang of teen roughs. I remember stepping off the bus one afternoon when I was approached by two menacing teens asking me which gang I associated with, the Dahms or the Weiners? In my typical Milquetoast manner, I said, "which gang are you with? I'm with you." Well it turns out that perhaps 15 boys from each gang had gathered on opposite sides of the alley looking for a showdown. I doubt there were any weapons, but physical hurt was probably intended. I was thankful that an adult hero entered the middle ground and talked the boys down. I know of no other such episodes in our community. And I don't know what happened to Brucie. Maybe he became a politician.

B-B guns

We must discuss B-B guns. Whatever possessed my dad to allow us B-B guns and pistols is beyond me. Dad was ordinarily very conservative in manners and methods. He wouldn't let us play football because of the risks for concussion. Red Ryder B-B guns were advertised heavily and kids I knew had them.

Grant & Ron defend our yard with Red Ryder B-B guns

B-Bs travel at 200 mph and can pierce skin. I was dumb and glad to get one for Christmas. It was like being a real cowboy in Dayton, Ohio. Tin cans and bottles were knocked off of walls. A pigeon or two succumbed to B-B death. Unfortunately, B-B misuse expanded beyond that.

Mr. Herolzer got hit in the neck as we were shooting in the neighborhood. George Beemsterboer's mother's insurance had to pay for a neighbor's bay window for the same reason. Mike Barlow spotted an old car in the brush, and thinking it was junk, we shot some of the windows out. We got a ride home in a police car because the owner claimed he was rehabilitating the car. Worst of all, Bob Homewood and I once decided (super dumb) to have a battle. From 30 yards, the very first shot from Bob hit me in the right forehead. Ever since, the memory of that moment sends shivers down my spine. My future could have been destroyed by loss of an eye.

And to make matters worse, multiple kids in the neighborhood owned B-B pistols and wandered about, occasionally shooting each other. B-B pistols shot smaller rounds with less velocity that stung but wouldn't pierce skin (but probably could take out vision). I will never fathom any reason for such toys.

Something almost as ludicrous was the day the Deger kids started throwing marbles at each other in the house, which led to the infamous case of the shattered full-length hall mirror. The older boys started the fracas and the "steelie" I threw at Ron broke the mirror. I insisted that we all should pay, and I got away with it.

Radio, TV, and Telephones

A major source of entertainment in those times was the radio. I would race home after school to listen to a succession of half-hour programs like The Adventures of Sky King and Jack Armstrong the All-American Boy. On Saturday mornings our imaginations could run wild with the stories of the Jungle Boy or Tarzan sponsored by Cream of Wheat cereals. Sunday nights held great fun on radio with comedy shows by Jack Benny, Bob Hope, Bing Crosby, Phil Harris, George Burns, Fibber McGee and Molly, the Great Gildersleve, and Amos & Andy. There was no sex, cursing, violence, gangster rap, or drugs on these programs. These were wholesome family products with huge appreciative audiences. Our local library sponsored readings of books to children by the librarians on Saturday mornings. Bowling was big. Even taking the family to the roller rink was in. Pea-shooters, hula-hoops, balsa wood model airplanes with rubber band powered propellers, and sling shots were in. Goods Hobby Shop on Main Street supplied some of those items.

Television didn't arrive for our family until 1950. I remember watching with fascination and jealousy a football game or a western movie at the Reilings before that. But our TV finally came by jeep during a snow storm. We were mesmerized by everything connected to television. We'd even watch the test pattern, which was screened before the programming began at 6 AM and finished at 11 PM. In fact, in the early days, TV programs may have only been available from 9 AM to 5PM. Howdy Doody, Buffalo Bob, Princess Summer-Fall-Winter-Spring, Flubadub, and Clarabelle the Clown were our favorite afternoon characters. And of course, there were dozens of Western movies featuring Roy Rogers (King of the Cowboys and oddly born in Portsmouth, Ohio), Gabby Hayes, Gene Autry (the Singing Cowboy), The Lone Ranger, and Hopalong Cassidy. In one movie, Hopalong was down the hill below a bad guy shooting down at him with a Gatling gun (sort of a machine gun with a revolving barrel). Hopalong was hit in the shoulder but nevertheless routed the evil one, jumped on his horse and rode triumphantly back to camp as if nothing had happened. Lucky for Hopalong it was just a movie.

Telephone service for most people was by party line, meaning several other houses might be sharing your line. Protocol dictated that you would wait until they were finished, but like the internet today, I suspect some people's privacy was violated. We had a single line because Dad was a doctor. It is odd that I can still remember Herb Clemens' number RA (Randolph) 9349, and John Jauch's number RA 4763. Our family number was RA 9892. No wonder I am forgetting things now that I am in my late 70s. There is just too much useless data floating around in my oligodendroglia (brain cells).

We were now Grant, Ronnie, Bobby, Chrissy, and Paula, when third sister Elizabeth Claire arrived June 6, 1950. We could now add Bethie at the end of the litany of children. Our parents granted us full access to the entire neighborhood, realizing we would return when hungry. I am not certain that safety was sacrosanct, but all of us did survive to adulthood with limbs, eyes, fingers, cranium, and gonads intact. Recall the episode of the "Great B-B Gun Shoot-Out" earlier. Every square meter of Kenwood, Kenilworth, and Delaware Avenues was our domain. Much of Dayton View in general was fully explored as well. At our block, there was no cross road connecting the parallel streets of Kenilworth and Delaware. Instead, there was a small dirt path with a rapidly rising four-foot berm punched through the forested green space between the two streets. What a great place for jumping one's bicycle. Kenilworth Avenue sloped downward above the berm. A determined run and sudden left turn in to the jump yielded an exhilarating short shot into space. Later we expanded on the idea by setting a plank on bricks further down Kenilworth for a longer run downhill and a greater aerial experience.

Now I must tell you of the "Peach Tree" episode. This was one of those shifting alliances where Rob was on the outs. Ron and I ganged up on nine-year-old Rob, stripped him naked on a cold day, and forced him under pain of great pain to run out to the peach tree in the backyard. That's all. But I had to tell it because it has been part of the family lore for decades. Ron has been called "Peach" ever since.

Mother was a saint. She was constantly cooking and washing dishes. I often joke about the culinary customs of those days.

"Oh good, Grant's home! Add some more water to the swill." But as previously indicated, mom could really put on a classic dinner for festivities. Mother refused to use a dishwasher even later when we had one. She thought it was easier to just wash and rinse and get it over with. All were supposed to have a week at the sink helping Mom dry and set away the dishes. I fear the older boys were not as dependable as they should have been. Can you imagine that mother never experienced the ease of microwaves, nor prepared vegetables, wraps, fruits, and hors d'oeuvres from Costco?

We were anything but derelicts, however. We all had jobs after grade school. I mentioned shoveling snow for neighbors. We made plaster statues from rubber molds, colored them and (tried) to sell them to neighbors. I worked for Don Hershey, pharmacist, and owner of Don's pharmacy on the corner of Richmond & Delaware Avenues. I washed the drug store floors and removed chewing gum from under the soda counter at 6 AM Sunday mornings. I whipped up cherry cokes (5 cents for the coke in a glass with ice and 1 cent for the flavoring), ice cream cones, malted milk shakes, and dispensed in-house products. When men asked to purchase condoms, I quietly demurred, and summoned Don from the back to make the sale. It was my understanding that good Catholics would not participate in selling condoms. Compared to pharmacies today, Don did well if he had 5–15 prescriptions to fill daily. He had a mortar and pestle to grind pills, make ointments, etc.

One tottery old lady from the neighborhood would come nightly to buy a double-deck vanilla cone. She would ask me to put a napkin over it, so she could transport her treat to eat at home. I admit to occasionally sampling from Don's variety nut display, which was supplied by Dayton Nut Products, a company owned by an uncle of my friend Walt Reiling.

I also worked summers at Phillips public swimming pool in their snack shack. The coke syrup and the root beer concentrate looked exactly the same. One day I created a turmoil because customers were complaining about cokes tasting like root beer. Evidently, I mistakenly poured the root beer concentrate into the Coke machine. Worse yet my boss caught me in the walk-in freezer with my finger in the huge can of vanilla soft-serve ice cream concentrate. My work was diligent but lacked certain refinements.

I learned to aggressively market my newspaper route. The paper boys assembled at Mrs. Treon's garage on Victor St., where the Dayton Daily News dumped hundreds of papers. I started with a fixed route of about 40 clients but built up to 72 customers. I watched when people moved into the apartment buildings we served and was the first to ask for their patronage. I was in Rick Treon's territory when Rick and I were wrestling in front of the door of a newly arrived apartment dweller. When the new renter opened the door, she gave me the contract because I was on top of Rick and she saw me first. On Sundays the paper was at least twice the size of the daily version. Added in were extra Sunday-only subscribers as well. I loaded 72 big papers into my canvas newspaper bag and placed them in the carrier over the front wheel of my bike. Then I filled the two side-saddle-bags over the back wheel. It was all I could do to push my poor heavily laden bike up Niagara Avenue hill to my apartments. I could work the six-unit apartments quickly by throwing folded newspapers to the two downstairs units, the two main level units, and the two balcony suites while hardly moving from the main entrance. It was embarrassing to throw a paper up over the railing to a second-floor customer and knock over their glass milk bottles. Once a bottle broke. Oh well, business is sometimes messy. Don't cry over spilt milk.

Budding work ethic

Speaking of bottles, we had one rather unsuccessful kissing party in the eighth grade. I think it was held in the Brogan's large basement. Roberta Klosterman called her mother to see if she would be allowed to participate. Most of us were painfully shy, but Sandra Hunt was the first to volunteer to "spin the bottle" (an empty glass milk bottle). Just about the time we were gaining confidence in the game, Susie Hook spun the bottle so hard that it broke, and the game dissolved.

Cub Scout and Boy Scout troops were sponsored by our parish and were excellent socializing and camping experiences with a great touch of patriotism and family support. My mother helped me construct a suit of knight's armor for a Cub Scout event. We covered cardboard with aluminum foil. We even made a helmet and cardboard sword to match.

Cub scouts in aluminum armor: back right Mom and her great friend Mrs. Dorothy Reiling; Ron & Grant opposite ends of the front row - 1949

During my time as a Boy Scout, I was not yet focused on climbing the ranks and mostly had fun. I learned to tie knots (square-knot, slip-knot, granny knot, figure of eight, sheet bend, clove hitch, bowline), cook a potato in hot embers, identify trees, and hike all over the place guided by a compass. At a regional scout meeting in Greenville, Ohio, we learned how to make rope, throw a spark with a flint, and start a fire, and to trade incidentals with scouts from around the region.

Grant at National Boy Scout Jamboree, Irvine Ranch, California - 1953

My parents gave me a wonderful gift in sending me by train to the 1953 Irvine, California, National Scout Jamboree in the summer of my eighth grade. Walt Reiling and John Duchek joined me from our Dayton troop. Bob Hope, Dorothy Lamour, and Roy Rogers entertained the 50,000 scouts who showed up. Trading posts from every state in the union offered trinkets of all kinds. I still have a dime radiated at the Oak Ridge Tennessee reactor. I've since lost a scout bandanna from Wyoming. We hauled water in five-gallon cans to our troop tents for drinking and cooking. We got a lot of woodfire ashes in our scrambled eggs, but we ate the mixture with gusto, possibly benefitting from the mineral supplements therein. They took us swimming in the ocean, which was a first for me. Train travel in those days was often spectacular. The mountains of Colorado, and the high plains of Arizona and New Mexico opened me to a whole new understanding of the greatness of the United States.

Grade school ended for me in 1953. Lifelong friendships had been formed. Over decades I could return to Dayton and whip up a party among the old gang. At this writing (2018) it is telling that any illness in one of our old buddies (now 79 years old) initiates an internet alert of questions, responses, prayers, and best wishes. Sadly, Vic King passed away two years ago, and we all contributed a very nice memorial for him at an Abbey he had served as architect for an expansion program. Last year, Judge Jim Brogan survived a six-vessel cardiac by-pass and thankfully survived. Walt Reiling endured three weeks in the intensive care unit before later passing on. I've recently commented to my wife Candice about our social life. It seems we either attend 80th birthday parties or funerals.

Phil and Doug racing a new train, Christmas - 1963

My fourth and fifth brothers Philip Joseph November 4th, 1955 and Douglas William April 30, 1957 completed the "Great Eight" sequence of Grant, Ronnie, Bobby, Chrissy, Paula, Bethie, Philip, and Dougie. Once when mom was exasperated, she said, "Grant, why don't you take Ronnie, Bobby, Chrissy, Paula, Beth, Philip 'n Doug somewhere?"

What a bunch! We really filled up the family 1951 Ford Country Squire station wagon, which proudly featured real wood slats on the sides. We filled the dining room table with laughter and jokes. On Sundays we had family dinners fairly regularly, and often with grandparents, relatives, and dates, and always on Thanksgiving, Christmas, and Easter. And we really did fill up 617 Kenilworth.

By the time I was approaching 16, it was embarrassing to still be a paperboy. So, Vic King, Bill Pflaum, and I started "Newlawn Yard Service." We put a hitch on my 1947 Chevy, built a trailer over an old Ford axle, purchased two gas lawn mowers, rakes, clippers, trimmers, and business cards and went to work. We printed our motto on our business cards, to wit: "No Lawn Like Newlawn." We often cut, raked, and then recut, yielding a postcard-perfect lawn. I was very good at clipping a straight hedge. People would see the vigor and quality of our work and ask us if we could do their lawns. For three years we were quite busy. $2.75 per person per hour was our request and we got it. We had several $20 yards. Bill was the organizer and got good customers from connections in well-to-do Oakwood. Our best customer asked us if we could plant myrtle. "Sure," we said. Vic and I raced to the library to learn what myrtle was. Vic didn't even know which end of the plant went in the ground. I told him to put the roots in first. A lady customer would often offer us something to drink. I couldn't stand beer like my peers did, so I took her offer of cranberry juice. I am pleased that it took me more than 60 years to learn to like beer. It saved me a lot of trouble.

A word or two about my beloved 1947 Chevrolet... It was dishwater brown, had full race windshield wipers and was shaped somewhat like a turtle. It had over 95,000 miles on the speedometer when I purchased it in 1955 from my next-door neighbor. Mr. Kauffman had taken the old car to Michigan to hunt deer, so I had to clean some fur out of the trunk. Young folks might be amazed that it had no electric turn signals. To show my directional intentions I had to roll down the window and make hand signals. The shift system was called a vacuum shift (it was really difficult to shift unless the motor was running). The high-beam lights button was on the floor above and to the left of the gear shift. The front grill had an open space for a hand crank if needed, but I never used it. The fenders rattled at 35 miles per hour, alerting various girlfriends to my approach. Cecil Shirk and I changed the muffler and the brakes once. I installed turn signals from a kit later. I was on a date one Saturday night when the odometer turned precisely 100,000 miles. I stopped the car on Main St. to gaze at this automotive achievement. It was an emotional moment for me, although my date thought I was a bit weird.

Our Third Home

Our third home featured a full landscaped lot on the left side

In 1957 when I was finishing high school, we moved to 724 Kenilworth Avenue, the last of the full-measure Deger family homes. Mom and Dad later moved to Knollwood Ave., further north and east near Main Street. Sadly, most of their retiring generation was moving to the more upscale southern Dayton suburbs of Oakwood, Kettering, and Centerville. Nevertheless, 724 Kenilworth Avenue was really a pleasant place. It gloried in two stories, an attic, and a basement, a screened-in porch, and a double yard. There was a high cedar border on the east side, trees in the yard, a shed and garage. There was more living space, but remember there were ten humans living in it. The three older boys slept upstairs on the old sun porch. Nothing wrong with that except several of the windows and the sills did not seal. The room could get below freezing in wintertime. Once a small pile of snow formed on the floor under the corner window near my bed. My two younger brothers got electric heating blankets for winter, but I refused because I was no sissy. Maybe that's why I never grew tall like the rest of my family.

The adjoining room held the older boys' desks and closet. The humble clothing of three teenaged boys was crammed into the closet. I was the eldest and at the same time the shortest. My lot in life was not to buy new clothes but to wear the "hand-me-ups" from my two younger brothers.

724 Kenilworth was a fine estate, especially in summer. The wedding reception for my sister Chris was held in the side yard and was a magnificent event. Mrs. Charlotte Foy helped mom with the preparations. The day was bright and beautiful, as Ohio summers can be.

Christmas - 1963

Dad paid $29,000 for the house, and unfortunately 20 years later sold it for the same price. The neighborhood had deteriorated so rapidly due to demographic shifts that a place of decency descended into drug activity, slovenly neighbors, and in some cases boarded-up houses. But while the "Great Eight" lived there, it flourished. All the adventures of 617 continued only better.

Chaminade High School

But I must not get ahead of the story. High school days were fabulous. Chaminade H.S. was centrally located downtown and attracted approximately 1200 male students from the 12 surrounding Catholic grade schools. At that time, Dayton was a relatively large industrial city in its prime. Dayton's National Cash Register Company manufactured cash registers for the entire world. Dayton engineer/inventors patented electric starters for cars, Delco automobile paints, and flip-top lids for aluminum cans. Orville and Wilbur Wright solved the problems of flight and gave aviation to the world. Mead Paper Company created utility papers for the whole country and published magazines with national distribution. Hundreds of small businesses produced springs, scales, pumps, and boiler parts. Vic King's dad was accountant for the Gustaf Widike Company, which made pressure relief valves for boilers. Dayton was an economic dynamo. It was often joked about town that Kentucky schools taught the "Three R's," Readin', Ritin', and the Road to Dayton.

Chaminade had the best football team in the city and almost in the state, the best pre-game rallies, and the best education in the city. We were descendants of Italians, Poles, Hungarians, Hispanics, and Germans. Black students were well liked and joined seamlessly in all of the many school-based activities. We were all friends in the best sense. We were all Americans with no hyphens. We shared a common Faith. We laughed heartily at ethnic jokes before the world was socially correct. Social correctness today seems to be causing a lot of divisiveness. Glad we missed out on that "improvement."

Note that I said the school was male only. That would seem odd in today's world, but frankly the distractions were fewer, and the education superior. Teenage guys have a wonderful sense of humor and comradery. Furthermore, there was nothing more stirring than 1200 male voices in the gym, sounding out for our team in a pre-game pep rally. It was fun.

Chaminade was staffed by Marianist priests and brothers, serving others in the name of Mary, Mother of God. The founder of the Marianist order was Father William Chaminade, a French priest during the difficult times of their Revolution of 1789. His religious influence spread to the United States where Marianist high schools and colleges developed in New York, Hawaii, and Dayton.

The males of the Deger "Great Eight" took the bus from Salem Avenue, transferred at Five Oaks, and headed downtown to the bus stop in front of Borchers Ford. BJ Borchers was the son of the owner of the dealership. The first model Thunderbird came to Borchers Ford in 1954. It had two seats, a hearty roar, a low sleek sexy look, and a base price of $2700. It impressed me, but apparently not BJ. He became a member of the Marianist order. Borchers Ford donated driver training cars to Chaminade.

As a freshman entering Chaminade in September,1953, I was called to the office of the principal, Brother Matthew Betz SM, for a personal interview. I was frightened enough about meeting with someone so high up but was frantic when I got lost trying to find his office. Turns out he was kind and just wanted to greet each new student. Brother Charles Eckhardt SM was Dean of Boys. The SM designation stands for Society of Mary. Brother Tragaser was the band director. I applied to join the band since I was too small for basketball and football. The good brother said, "We will try you out on the piccolo." That didn't work. "Your lips are too fat," he said. He offered me a sousaphone (a tuba with wrap-around tubes suitable for marching). Fans loved to try to throw popcorn, gum wrappers, and other small missiles down the broad opening of the sousaphone. I stuck with the sousaphone for the full four high school years.

Sousaphones make great targets for wads of paper, gum, popcorn, & candy wrappers

There is an old 8mm film of one of our Thanksgiving football games when we ranked high in the state. At half-time our band was executing a difficult marching program with great precision, until one of the sousaphone players darted out 180 degrees in the wrong direction. I won't tell you the name of that band member.

Our green and white band uniforms were snappy, with a large white tassel sticking up from the tall regimental hats. I think the girls liked the uniforms too. At least the Julienne girls (Catholic girls' high school on the other side of town) liked to parade about in front of us during the football games. Leading the energetic Chaminade student body in boisterous songs and cheers from our front row seats was magical.

Chaminade won every football game in the city my first year and went on to second place in the State of Ohio, losing to Massillon. Our band also marched on public streets celebrating the annual Holy Name parade. I suppose a religious parade on public streets would cause civil unrest today. We played for the Archbishop when he visited Chaminade. I recall Brother Tragaser, our director, kneeling before the bishop to kiss his Apostolic ring. The band also played on stage for our yearly Spring Concert.

Holy Name parade 1954

I was fairly excited about everything. Even the school lunches amazed me. I could always expect a full portion. At home one's food was at risk if you were called to the phone. Some sibling would clean your plate. Portions of entrees would sometimes simply run out while sharing food with seven other hungry Deger kids. I was excited about the bowling team. Walt Reiling, Dick Treon, John Jauch, Bob Homewood, and I won the intramural Bowling League championship our sophomore year. We called our team "The Alley Cats." I was excited about the football rallies held in the gym. These exercises in school solidarity were big, funny, and really noisy. It seemed like we were going to lift the ceiling up. Our athletes were cheered, and they usually won their games. I joined the Sodality, a prayer group expounding good behavior and ethical leadership. I was an academic Honor Roll and National Honor Society member.

No one today would consider taking four years of high school Latin as I did. Latin is a long dead language, except for use in church, sacred music, and learned documents. A small population in southern Switzerland still speaks the language. But I've got to tell you, all my life I've had a hands-up ease understanding words because of their Latin derivatives. When William, a Norman Frenchman, conquered Harold's Anglo-Saxon England in 1066, French merged into the English language. In time, 40% of the English vocabulary contained essentially Latin-French derived words. And of course, in the freshman year of medical school one has to learn 13,000 new words, most of which have Latin origins. Try to understand the muscle "extensor hallucis longus" without appreciating Latin. That muscle extends the big toe. Prescriptions were formally written in Latin, and today still contain abbreviations derived from Latin. For example, if your prescription says to take this pill qd, you are to take it *quaque die*, or every day. If the loudspeaker blasts, "Dr. Jones to the Emergency Room, stat," you know that stat comes from Latin *statim*, immediately! The word Concupiscence is totally derived from Latin, because Romans were real Latin lovers.

There were some dark corners in our community. One acquaintance was heavily bearded in the eighth grade. His father was said to have underworld connections. If we brought firecrackers named "lady fingers" or 1-inch firecrackers, he brought cherry bombs and 180s to the alleys where we blew them up. His bombs could launch a metal trash can several feet in the air. Another student friend was a skinny kid, but in high school he could drink a bottle of beer for every inning of a Cincinnati Red-Legs double-header. Amazing!

Another of our high school acquaintances had money, an addiction to alcohol, and a new Cadillac. He drove weekends to a gambling club in Covington, Kentucky. He died of cirrhosis when I was a medical intern in Dayton in 1966. He was a friend of Howard's, who also had an alcohol problem. Jim would sometimes join us at Howard's home where we were trying to help each other with trigonometry. He would bring a bottle of whiskey and share it with Howard. Walt and I left to go to the corner drugstore to get a milkshake. Howard said he wanted to go with us. As we left the drugstore with our shakes, we momentarily lost track of Howard. We found him sitting bowlegged like an Indian Chief, leaning against the pharmacy building. It was obvious we had to help him home. It started to rain. As we struggled up the hill in the alley to his home, it became more difficult to keep him upright. Finally, he slid out of our grip to the ground. I'll never forget watching the rain wash over Howard's midsection like a little waterfall. We barely got him in his back door to the care of his family. A different friend reportedly died of AIDs in the early years of that disease. He was a distant friend and a good guy. No one knew of his preferences at the time, or more likely I knew little of the world.

Howard was a case study. He was uncommonly gifted, with an IQ well into the genius level. Unfortunately, the gift of brain-power does not necessarily come with a balanced personality. He was brisk, pushy, and overbearing with girls. He was often entertaining among the guys, but when he drank a lot, he became boorish. He would launch into an off-the-wall discussion of Herodotus, or hedonism, or the "Fall of the Roman Empire." He was fun to ice fish with on Indian Lake but would end up in a drunken drizzle. He also owned a '47 Chevy, a red one that was formerly a Fire Chief's car. One day he showed up at my house and commanded that I carefully and steadily hold this round melon-sized ball of plaster of paris while he drove to Five Oaks Park. He then cautiously took the ball from my hands and threw it into the air as far as he could. To my amazement, it exploded mid-air into tiny shards. He had put potassium permanganate into a small glass beaker, and then set a test tube of sulfuric acid in the beaker and covered the volatile ingredients in plaster. Holy mackerel! He could have seriously injured both of us. Another time he nearly burned down the cherry tree in his back yard testing a pipe bomb. Howard joined the military, bicycled the perimeter of Japan, neglected further education, rarely held longstanding jobs, and very slowly sank. The three of us who owned '47 Chevrolets (Vic, Howard, and me) went separate ways. I was spared the dark way and stayed with the great majority of my friends who were productive, positive, sober, and often responsible.

When the "Old Gang" gathers, we usually rehash some of the more notable capers. One was the adventure of the Combustion of the Christmas Trees. "It was a dark and lonely night" in winter. We gathered used Christmas firs and made a pile in the cement alley behind Walt's house. Someone lit the pile and it exploded with fury. Soon the flames were above the height of the garages. The Fire Department was called. Mrs. Klosterman, a widow with nine children, led her offspring in a real fire drill. Did I say that it was midnight on a cold night? No one was hurt, nor damage done, except for the cost of city services. The perpetrators had long since fled the scene. Walt later said that he recognized Mike Barlow's laugh from his bedroom.

Bowling with the boys on a weekend was a serious bonding event. John, Mike, Vic, and I were enjoying the comradery of a good match, when Vic abruptly decided to leave. We had reason to doubt his explanation that he needed his sleep. We suspected he wanted to visit his girlfriend, Judy Tidball. Sure enough, we later discovered his car (a 1947 Chevy, by the way) in front of Judy's house. Vengeance was required for breaking up the rituals of the brotherhood! John went to his home and brought back a jack. With that jack we raised the rear end of Vic's car ever so little, just enough to lift the rear tires above the surface of the road. We waited in hiding and eventually Vic got into his car to go home. He flailed the gear shift back and forth from first to reverse, without any ensuing motion. We were howling out loud in the dark and made no effort to solve his dilemma.

I have forgotten so many of our capers, but for your sake, dear readers, that is probably good. But I must tell you that after biology lab, someone did stuff a starfish arm in Jim Brogan's sandwich. Someone did tie a black string to a stick of blackboard chalk, which rested on the eraser track. When our aged trigonometry teacher Brother Jannings stiffly reached for the chalk to write, it moved a few inches down the track. When he reached again, it moved again, sort of like a stunt in a Groucho Marx movie. Jim Bernier and I laughed all through English poetry. We drew moustaches on the pictures of the great poets in our English literature text. One obviously Hell-bound classmate tied a condom to a light-switch string as Father Gerber was lecturing with scathing words about the serious spiritual sickness of concupiscence and the shamefulness of illicit sex (notice the alliteration). For those uninitiated in Latin, concupiscence means lust.

I was so well taught at Chaminade High School that college and medical school were easy transitions. I was beginning to take life seriously and started to pile up some good grades. I enjoyed freshman algebra because I could quickly solve the problem in my head. I was often first to raise my hand with answers. Chemistry, biology, and physics released the great mysteries of life, and I wanted more.

University of Dayton

My college was the University of Dayton, a coed Catholic University, founded by the Marianist Priests and Brothers, the same order that taught at my high school. I was 17 when I started college in 1957. In those days, tuition costs were $15 per credit hour. I would take 20 credits per semester for $300. Finishing college in four years was expected and completed. My dad paid most of the tuition, and I paid maybe $150 a semester for books. I supported my car, a cigarette habit, and saved a lot of money by living at home. I almost always held a job, usually working evenings as a laboratory technician at Good Samaritan Hospital. Sometimes I took laboratory night-call, in a small room above the chapel. I was paid $12 per night to be roused for emergency blood tests in cases of hemorrhage or diabetic crisis, or cross-matching units of blood for injury victims, or spinal fluid studies for suspected meningitis.

College students were probably 85% male, especially where engineering, science, and premedical studies were concerned. Now women on campus outnumber men. I rarely dated classmates. More often I asked girls from local parishes, or from the nursing school at Good Samaritan Hospital where

I worked, to join me for a movie, a New Year's party, a dance, or a prom. We usually double dated.

Buoyed up by such excellent high school preparation and very good high school grades, I proceeded with confidence. Contrary to the problem so many students have at matriculation time, I already knew my path. I wanted to be a doctor. I carefully chose my math, chemistry, and biology topics in logical progressive fashion and never looked back. Some students would shift majors, just because the matriculation line for History was shorter than the one for Sociology, for example. I noticed that indecision was readily assuaged by having served in the military. Some of my old high school friends who were floating in life returned from active duty with a firm sense of determination. These former soldiers were darned good competitors and had seen enough of hard reality to know that education meant much to them. And they had the GI Bill to help them.

May I offer my thoughts about why college is proportionately so expensive in 2018 compared to 1957? My alma mater, the University of Dayton, was singularly dedicated to the essentials of education: lecture halls, labs, and dormitories segregated by gender. Luxuries did not exist. Yes, we did have a football field, and Brother Paul's greasy spoon sandwich shop. A surplus WWII Quonset Hut served as a recreational center, featuring a few pool tables and card tables.

Today by contrast, every university purchases great swaths of real estate around it. Universities cultivate bucolic landscaped grounds, mimicking the works of "Capability" Brown, a 17th Century Englishman who designed classic English estates, like Blenheim for the Duke of Marlborough. Today universities build Olympic swimming pools, elaborate exercise facilities, multiple sport complexes, 24-hour dining services, bowling alleys, theaters, gathering spaces to sing Kum-Bay-Ya in, and hire faculty to promote political correctness. They even construct spaces for students upset by socially incorrect talk to have a massage and a talk with a psychologist. Good grief, no wonder college is too expensive today. And I'm not even sure they learn as well as we did. Things were simpler then. Consider that students today need to pack around laptop computers, cell phones, and calculators. In our day, engineering students used slide rules for mathematical calculations. Slide rules were made of wood, were very accurate, and probably cost a dozen dollars. And we saved a lot of time by not incessantly tweeting what we ate for breakfast, or where the next social activist meeting is being held.

I loved college. I got highs from doing very well in exams, and exploring the secrets of biology, chemistry and physics. I had been well prepared by my Catholic high school education for the discipline and excitement of learning. I was too much of a nerd, and very motivated to reach my goal (and earning enough money to do so). I was rarely enticed by drinking, parties, wild weekends, etc. I didn't have time or cash for such diversions. I rarely even went to our home football games or attended our nationally recognized winning basketball team games. I was busy. I always had a job, especially working as a lab tech at Good Samaritan Hospital evenings. One semester I got a 4-point grade average (all As) while working 40 hours per week and taking 20 credit hours. Somehow, I found time to date a number of great young ladies but knew that I had a lot to do before I got serious. I probably missed a lot by contemporary standards, but in the long term everything worked out wonderfully well.

Peter J. Faso, PhD, was our freshman biology professor. Like so many UD teachers, he was well versed, entirely confident in his sphere, and railed on in unnecessarily wordy sentences, drawn out like W.C. Fields would have done. To quote Dr. Faso, "Behold this mosquito species, Aedes aegipti, a member of the ubiquitous arthropod class, whose insidious swarms do so terrorize the temperate regions of mother earth, inflicting untold disease and death upon homo sapiens." I remember getting 100% on his biology exam because I was one of the few who could answer an add-on question, "How does a hydra walk?" The answer came from a footnote at the bottom of the many pages we were to study from our text. A hydra (a quite tiny aquatic animal) stands on its stem and leans over onto one of its stick-like arms and then rolls over onto its head, the other arm, and then again onto its stem. Neat huh?

Dr. Carl Michaelis taught freshmen chemistry. He was another of our pre-med mentors who was so artful at explaining his course matter. Later, medical school just didn't seem difficult, because I was so well prepared. Physics and higher math did not come easily, but with determination I was able to keep the grade point average up.

Walt Reiling was my close and best friend all through college. We took the same pre-med courses, studied together, and worked together in the clinical lab at Good Samaritan Hospital after school. Walt was clearly the more gifted. He was ultimately the first in the Science Division at graduation and went on to Harvard Medical School. I was ninth in the division of 465 students. But we really studied well together. I would generally take more thorough classroom notes. But Walt grasped the big picture and could explain what it all meant better. Our process was: 1. study on our own, 2. meet to correlate and correct our notes, 3. quiz each other, and 4.

take turns doing the math or writing chemical structures on the blackboard. We were so efficient at doing the routine preoperative urinalyses and blood counts for the hospital that we would often have time to study at the laboratory's blackboard. Bernie Liddy, who also worked at the lab, often joined us. He was a year ahead of us and became a physician as well.

I was accepted to the four medical schools I applied to. I asked my father which one he would recommend. In typical fashion he asked, "Which one is the cheapest?" The University of Cincinnati Medical School's fees were less because of support by both city and state. Ever since I had a paper route, I had saved for medical school. And I always took on outside employment every year of my school days from high school on. I graduated from a fine medical school without debt. I took a rotating internship at Good Samaritan Hospital in Dayton, and an internal medicine residency at Mayo Clinic in Rochester, Minnesota. I served in the Air Force as a Captain in the medical corps for two years at Fairchild Air Force Base (a SAC Headquarters with nuclear weapons on B-52s) during the Viet Nam War. I'm happy to report that I helped keep Spokane, WA, free of the communist hoards during my service. And by the way, I finally quit smoking cigarettes. A few more years with a pipe and I was free.

Why Washington State?

I have mused long and often why The Grant Branch of the eight Ohio siblings ended up in Washington State. Was it due to my mother's red Sunday hat? It was big. The brim was big, like Saturn's rings. Mother would lead the charge up the center aisle of our parish church with her ducklings falling in behind, the tallest to the shortest. It was like the Mickey

Mouse Club being led by a spaceship. She was proud, oh so proud, of her large and growing brood. But as the eldest child, I was quite self-conscious and felt as if everyone was watching. I can tell you that mother was greatly loved and always will be, but she was a commanding presence that spilled over into a lot of my life. After the passage of time, I realize more and more that her admonitions and suggestions were given with great love and amazing sagacity. She was almost always on the mark. Did I move away to avoid the red spaceship? I doubt it. I still get to Dayton every year or two. All of us have kept in close touch over all these years. I consider Ohio my real home. Mothers don't give up on your children! They don't get smart as rapidly as you might like. But they always love and admire you.

My wife Peg and I had simply agreed to strike out for a new life after I finished residency and my Air Force duty. Thanks to serving in the military, we fell in love with Washington State. We learned to ski and camp, and fish for trout. We dug clams on the coast and watched the waves roll in. We scouted the mountain trails, the sub-alpine lakes and waterfalls, and learned to name the mountain flowers. We soon had three really great kids.

The Brothers Three on Tour

In October 1999, I joined brothers Ron and Rob for several days of traveling in Ohio together. We revisited many sites of our shared Ohio memories. This is the story of our trip, which I had recorded. Rob dug up a copy of my notes and suggested inclusion in this book.

So here is that story.

I'll tell you about our brotherly adventure, set in 1999, reliving childhood vacations of nearly 50 years ago. I'll tell you of visions of the Ohio scene, including the spirits of past and present. I'll tell you of farms, friends, families, flea markets, churches, reliquaries, cemeteries, city halls, and a special autumnal hike (in the wrong direction). I will tell you of Deger ancestry. I will tell you that it was good. It was all good.

Friday, October 22
The morning comes quickly when speeding east on the "Red Eye" flight from Seattle at 560 mph. But I slept well on that portion of the flight until Detroit greeted me at 3:23 AM. My watch still said 12:23 AM Pacific Time. I was pumped and ready to go when Ron picked me up in Dayton at 8 AM EST.

Ron probably has amassed a PhD equivalency in genealogy. We had barely pulled away from the airport ticket booth before he was telling me of a recent find of interest to our Clan. A one Larry Deger was the Marshall of Dodge City, who served for a while with Wyatt Earp. While our Larry never made the major history books, he was a major figure in his day. Larry was a 19th century German farmer and saloon keeper, and weighed over 300 lbs. (truly a major figure).

I was immediately infatuated with Ron's new home in Kettering. Its winding road and driveway were covered with brightly colored red, yellow, and orange fallen deciduous leaves. The grounds were high and looked down toward the Dayton Country Club golf course. I loved the house's attractive stone work, the guest annex apart from the main house, and a pastoral neighborhood that would be anyone's pride.

Rob had driven up from Louisville and joined us at Ron and Joyce's home. Our bags were gathered and suddenly we were off to lead the life of the Three Amigos, City Slickers, Musketeers, and Pants-less Brothers*! (*See the story of the Peach Tree earlier in this book.) There must have been a touch of mystery in the blowing autumn winds and the swirling skies. Those breezes seemed to say, "Elders of the Clan Deger, you are called to discover your lore and share it with your kinfolk." And so, we begin.

No trip to Dayton is fulfilled without a trip to Calvary Cemetery, which holds the earthly remains of our beloved parents and many relatives. A trip to Calvary refreshes the vision and voices of Dad and Mom. I always touch the headstones as if Dad and Mom were once again holding my hand at 1325 Salem Avenue. I always shed a tear or two for want of their advice and caring. But in a minute, I'm telling jokes and thinking of happy things, because I was so very happy with them.

Nearby Carillon Park holds memories of Grandfather Urban Deger who played those massive carillon bells from a keyboard on Sunday afternoons in his role as master musician in the community. Ron was anxious to give us a tour of the park and spiel off his vast knowledge of its history. In its community center, Rob and I purchased a small book of the poems of Paul Lawrence Dunbar, Dayton's son and renowned black author. Ron led us in a reading of Dunbar's lyrical "A Negro Love Song," written at the turn of the century. Mr. Dunbar received national recognition and his home is preserved as a place of interest. Dunbar High School in Dayton reflects his importance here.

Time was precious. We flew by Chaminade High School, our once male-only Catholic high school (now co-ed). We passed by the once-protective Cyoda Club building (CYO = Catholic Youth Organization) where we danced on Friday nights with well-chaperoned Catholic girls to the hits of the middle and late 1950s. Do you remember "Falling Leaves"? My heart still leaps a bit. Mostly I spent the evening gawking across the crowded hall instead of actually dancing. I would generally see someone I would like to ask to dance and falter, promising myself that I would ask her next week.

It was great to see the unique Dayton electric trolley cars again. They pick up power from the lines above the trolley. In my school days these busses were always full of passengers. They were early models of non-polluting vehicle power. Ron and I started telling Bill Clinton jokes, and Rob in return besmirched Republican claims with rapid-fire and telling wit. Ribald songs and ditties had their moment as we left the city for the countryside.

Rural Ohio doesn't seem to change. There was still a covered bridge to be seen. The family farms are still large and prosperous. The tiny towns with their small hardware stores, their large neighborhood pubs, their larger churches, and their huge porches for sitting outdoors in the summer to watch not much of anything go by, are still very much in evidence. Gas is 15 cents per gallon cheaper here than on the West Coast. An Amish couple drove by in their horse-drawn buggy. A nearby road sigh said, "DEER PROCESSING and HARNESS SHOP."

Well, something major did change in the last half century. The DeGraff Creamery had closed. Even without our usual superb ice cream treat, our intrepid spirit remained undaunted. We were soon at the headwaters of the great Miami River, which is given life by that rather large man-made body of water called Indian Lake.

Indian Lake was 60 miles north of Dayton, and probably the only rational vacation site for eight children of particularly hard-working 1950s era parents. It was close to Dayton, and it had rental cabins large enough to hold our gang. And we all fit into mom's bulky red 1951 Ford Country Squire station wagon with real wooden sideboards. We would sing scores of verses of "I've been Working on the Railroad" and "My Grandfather's Clock" and "A Hundred Bottles of Beer on the Wall," while squirming around and teasing our younger sisters. Dad and Mom's friends often arranged to cabin nearby. The Foys and the Reilings in particular added joy and similar aged kids to the grand melee. There were days of water skiing, swimming, fishing for perch, sunfish, and crappie, and outdoor picnics. The amusement park at Russell's Point was in operation in those years. I remember getting vertigo after a whirl on the Octopus. Phil was distraught when I threw up on his Sunday pants. Dad took roll upon roll of 8-mm movie film of the only week's rest he probably got all year. Years ago, I upgraded most of the films to VCR, but will need to convert them to DVD technology.

We located our motel for the next two nights. It is good that men are less concerned about minor details like cleanliness and comfort. I doubt if our wives would have put up with this place. The Villa Motel of Indian Lake, run by Gary Lynn & Judy Kay Boop, was not a glamorous place. The haymow of the A-frame structure held two single beds approached via a precipitous narrow stairway. A portion of the railing was missing and the carpet on the staircase was loose and dirty. Ron banged his toe pretty hard while managing the steep stairs. A separate bedroom was located on the main floor in the back near the water heater. The sink, stove, and refrigerator were almost clean. The two central lighting fixtures hanging from the apex of the ceiling were no longer functioning. At 9 AM the next morning, I went to the office to ask for new light bulbs. The manager was in his bathrobe and said he was too old to climb up to those light fixtures, but he'd send his son later when he woke up. "He usually gets up about noon," said Mr. Lynn.

But I've got to tell you, the A-frame was a great place for three mature brothers to play cards, drink whiskey, and tell tall tales. Euchre can really get one's blood running especially when hard-earned dimes are at stake. I wouldn't have passed up our two days in the Villa Motel for a fortune.

We found the Foy's old cottage on the first afternoon of our explorations of the lake. It still remains in their family. The amusement park at Russell's Point was replaced by rental condominiums with attached dock space. The statue of Our Lady of the Lake is still a landmark of the point overlooking the water from the southwest shore. We remembered seeing the statue as children. We found the area of Mr. Lou Emmelheinz's cottages from whom we rented the 1950s destination vacation home.

Which leads me to an insight into key interactions of the Brothers Three. We had decided to park the car and walk around some of the interconnected small islands on the northeastern shore of Indian Lake. We perambulated with abandon and lightheartedness several miles in many directions. We studied homes, docks, coves, bridges, water rushes, and waves. We watched an old man fishing from a tiny skiff near the bridge. We threw stones in the water and spoke of our vivid childhood memories of this very lake. In the same vicinity of our walk, Walt Reiling and I had swum across the lake. Another time, Walt and I were canoeing when he leaned over in the canoe to see what I was leaning over to see, and we both fell in.

The time to head back to our car arrived. I looked behind us and suggested that was the direction to go. Rob wasn't sure.

Ron made a take-command decision (as a good former Marine officer should) to proceed due forward. We trudged one-and-a-half to two miles in the absolutely wrong direction. On return to ground zero, we found our car a quarter of a mile behind us. It was cold and turning dark, but the walk enhanced my love for Ohio to the point of wishing to purchase one of these homes. Ron said he would cut the grass if I would purchase one of the lakeside homes and give him use of it in perpetuity. Rob humorously and sarcastically wondered if he could use the place to grow marijuana, perform abortions, and collect welfare checks, as good Democrats do.

Ron drifted through a stop sign and acquainted himself with the local constable. The officer was quite accommodating toward us city dudes and left Ron with just a warning. Dinner that night was a pile of steam-table food for less than $10, including the hot fudge sundae. The diner was within walking distance of our A-frame (as was the entire burg of Lakeview, Ohio 43331). I take a somewhat dim view on prioritizing "healthy eating." Like Johnny Carson once said, "I know a man who gave up smoking, drinking, sex, and rich food. He was healthy right up to the time he killed himself."

Saturday, October 23
It was my good fortune to win the downstairs bedroom for the first night. I was spared descending the staircase-of-doom for nocturnal toileting. And sure enough, Son-of-Bath-Robed-Manager did show up at noon to fix the light bulbs. He was a chap of some dexterity. He was able to replace the burned-out bulbs by hanging onto the decorative fan while standing on the remainder of the railing.

Breakfast at another of Lakeview's fine cafés turned out to be a culinary delight and bargain at $10 for the three of us. The waitress at Bud & Emily's Café was so pleasant that Rob left a generous tip. His recent life experiences caused him to forget that women can be pleasant, and he was definitely touched. The sky was clouded, the winds picked up, and the temperature dropped. It was the season for manly adventure.

We found Waterbury Rd. again where the Emmelheinz's cottages were located. They all remain but have been partially rebuilt and repainted so that we couldn't be absolutely certain which one we stayed in during several summer vacations prior to 1955. We then drove the circumference of this huge 8000-acre lake. There are many blue-collar developments with trailer homes for the weekend fisherman. But there are some very attractive homes on the numerous bays, islands, and coves off the north and east shores of the lake.

We read the real estate offerings and the for-sale signs as we toured the lake and its islands. A visitor from the expensive Northwest like myself could hardly believe the local bargains. A double mobile home on the waterfront with dock cost $55,000. A waterfront 3-bedroom home with dock, lift, deck, and pontoon boat sold for $129,000. In Bellingham, Washington, the lot alone would be more than that. At times I have wished I could just take the plunge, give up my exceedingly busy life, and go fishing in Ohio at Ohio prices.

During lunch at a classic red-neck joint called the Town Tavern, Ron discussed some genealogy of the Briggs family. Since the beers were only $1.25 each, we had time and money to listen to the intriguing tale of one Henry Mallow, who was the first child of European descent born in Ohio country. Ron wove a tapestry of ancestry to prove that Henry was also a relative of ours. (More on that later.)

We had enough of Indian Lake for the moment and headed due west to St. Henry and Maria-Stein, where Ron's wife

Joyce Neikamp's family originated. Steepled churches with crosses on top were everywhere, a witness to the Precious Blood order of priests and nuns who served the German Catholic immigrants from the 1870s onward. An ecclesiastical museum of their order at Maria-Stein (Mary of the Mountain) is to be found near New Bremen, OH, if my memory serves me correctly. Quietly dignified, the museum is surrounded by cultivated fields and large farms. The reliquary (chapel of relics of saints) is one of the striking religious museums to be found anywhere. First-class relics (e.g., pieces of bone or flesh) of some powerful saints (Francis of Assisi, for example) are contained in small brass medallions about the size of a small beeper and hung in display about the chapel walls. There is an alleged piece of the True Cross there as well. These items were brought to the United States for safety during a time of civil unrest in Italy.

We purchased some artifacts from the gift shop, dutifully attended by zealous women, who were quite pleased to welcome visitors to an otherwise fairly quiet place. I reviewed some of their albums and documents and found reference to Sister Vivian Ann Barga and Sister Willette Barga, postulates of the 1960s. St Charles seminary is only several miles away. There was a palpable presence of our Faith in this area, and it was good.

We found Joyce and John Deger at Mrs. Florentine Neikamp's farm house where we had a pleasant reunion. The tree swing from the tree by the garage is still functional. Then off to Neikamp's *Farm and Fleamarket on Route 127,* an amazing business created on the site of an old turkey farm. In warehouses where turkeys once fattened, mercantile booths now flourish. There are merchants hawking eclectic and diverse merchandise such as Amish furniture and gazebos, nuts and bolts, jams and jellies, lamps, guitars, antiques, aromatherapy candles, animal figurines, fresh fruits and vegetables, boiled eggs in vinegar, and of course, turkey products. Mr. Neikamp takes chances on selling sometimes obscure wares. But it was a great place to visit and see how the genre works.

Celina Lake at St. Mary's is larger than Indian Lake but hardly as colorful. We'd had enough traveling by now and returned to our Lakeview A-frame for euchre and whiskey and a short walk to the nearby steam-table for a $7.95 dinner with all the hot fudge and ice-cream one could ingest for the price. I lost 50 cents playing cards. And to make matters worse, I had to take one of the upstairs beds. I made two trips to the bathroom during the night, taking my life in my hands maneuvering down the steep and poorly handrailed stairs. I called it the Via Dolorosa.

Sunday, October 24

Back to Bruce and Emily's for $1.59 waffles and hot java. At the next table one old lady held forth to her lady friend across the table and jabbered for thirty minutes without stopping. We wondered how the quiet one could stand the barrage. We attended Mass at St. Mary of the Woods parish and there had a chance meeting with my good friend Walt and his wife Sue Reiling. The Reilings own a great place on the lake, a fine home on a choice corner waterway on an easy-to-get-to island on the lake. We spent an hour as their guests reminiscing, which was quite a treat for me.

Back to Dayton for dinner at Ron's with brothers Phil and his wife Terri, Doug, and Dad's friend Margaret Hayes. Joyce provided an excellent meal culminating in homemade apple pie….awesome! The assembled discussed the possibility of a general family reunion. Phil and I agreed to share planning for it as a committee with one of our sisters. With tremendous glee, we watched videotapes of our childhood, which provided food for remembering old Clan stories. A good time and a good night's sleep were had by all.

Monday, October 25
It was a hard sell to get Rob on the road by 8 AM, but it was the last day of our adventure and we wished to explore the Scioto River Valley, and in particular the seat of Mom's ancestry in Ross County. After all of that, Rob was faced with an additional three-hour drive back to his home in Louisville. Ron's son John joined the Brothers Three. His insights added to the combined wisdom of the Clan Elders. John relieved a moment of indecision by reminding us, "If you don't know where there is, you don't know when you've gotten there." That pearl was surely one of the greatest of the trip.

We identified the Charles Briggs farm and an old Methodist Church near Austin, Ohio. There a really old red one-room schoolhouse with a cornerstone dating to 1907 exists, where some of Mom's ancestors may have been educated. A larger building next door is labeled Austin Grad School. Both buildings lie fallow in a field. The larger one is almost, but not quite completely, compatible with a picture we have of Willa Briggs, Grandmother Vera Grant's sister, standing in front of her school. Ron has quite a collection of data, pictures, and maps of our mother's side of the family.

We added to our data bank at the Ross County Genealogical society and the Ross County Courthouse. Both sources of information provide an amazing experience if only for the opportunity to open up the past to one's view. You'd be surprised at the variety of documents. At the genealogical society's building, we found material compiled and submitted by people from all over the country who had Ohio roots. There were tomes sufficient to produce a PhD thesis. The Society makes no effort to correct mistakes but will publish corrections. We found, for example, that my grandmother Vera Grant's sister's name (Great Aunt Willa) was incorrectly spelled. At lunch in Chillicothe, Ohio, the conversation turned to the state of marriages in the 1990s. Pondering this, John came forth with another brilliant insight, "My ex-wife-to-be is out there somewhere." John is such a Clan treasure. He most certainly is our one and true Dalai Lama.

I promised you the skinny on how the Deger Clan could possibly be related to the first child of European descent to have been born in Ohio country. Well here it is.

A certain Henry Mallow was in utero when hostile Indians took his mother, sister Sarah, and brother Adam from their West Virginia farm in the 1750s. Sarah was murdered on the spot. The remaining captives were taken to the Ohio territory. In the Scioto Valley of Ohio near present-day Portsmouth, Ohio, Mrs. Mallow gave birth to Henry. Mother and new son were sold to French traders in New Orleans and about two years later escaped and made their way back to Pendleton County, Virginia (now West Virginia) and were reunited with their family. Henry stayed in West Virginia. His brother Adam, meanwhile, was raised as an Indian. He was released during a prisoner exchange in Philadelphia and returned to his home in Virginia. It took some time for him to relearn English and the ways of the colonists. Adam served in the Revolutionary War. He later moved to the Ohio area where he had been held prisoner. He grew to become a prosperous Ohio farmer.

Several generations later, a descendant of Henry's (whom you remember was born in captivity in Ohio) married Charles Briggs. Her name was Catherine Mallow. One of their sons was Rufus Briggs, who married Mary Irons. Rufus and Mary birthed seven red-haired and self-assured sisters, one of whom was my grandmother Vera (Briggs). Vera married Joseph Grant, and Winifred my mother was their second of three children.

This is the story of three good brothers who took joy in sharing their lives once again. All good stories must come to an end. Godspeed and blessing to all.

Grant

December 15, 1999

Goodbye Blest Mother

I wrote this piece shortly after Mother's death in 1992:

Winifred Grant Deger, age 75, died suddenly and peacefully February 5, 1992, while at breakfast with Robert, her husband of 53 years. She leaves eight children who freely give her homage, and almost adulation for her ability to love and guide our large family. Upon learning of her abrupt departure from my life, I wept bitterly. Yet as I sat to write about her, I found serenity in contemplating my privilege at having her for 52 years. So, I'm here with you to say goodbye no matter how hard it is to do. And I pray for the proper words to adequately portray her virtues.

She was probably the ultimate role model for the ideal mother. Mom was the soul and spirit of our family, the internal glue who made it all work. Moreover, she seemed to do it with comfort and ease, although it must have been an unbelievable vocation to feed, bathe, comfort, launder, bandage, diaper, listen to and oversee our large family and home. She was always there for us, day after year. She had few vacations; little help; no compensation package; no personal leave days or holidays; and can you believe, no complaints!!!

There was always balance. Each of us felt as if we were the most loved and desired in her eyes, but knew she had no favorites. She always developed deep sincere friendships: nothing superficial or pompous about her. She assumed you were her friend, and if you took the bait, she'd never let you down. She loved to laugh and to hear the stories of others. She had written a letter to my mother-in-law Ruth Zehnder, just before she died, and yesterday Ruth read it to me. I loved the cheery bright chatty words that flowed as she made her common world sound special to the reader.

I honestly don't think she knew how to swear. She possessed the fullness of expression and just didn't need to express such words. She didn't smoke or drink, except one Christmas Day she had a glass of Mogen David wine and glowed red-faced all day. She was too busy encouraging us, making us feel good to disparage others. Optimism and a go-for-it attitude never left her even after her own serious illnesses. As a child I never understood the concept of adversity or fear because my mother dwelt on none. It never occurred to us to steal, cheat, or lie in any major way because it wasn't what she taught, and Lord knows it was hard enough to keep up with her kind but perpetually high expectations. I guess she taught us the real ethics of life that we of the current generation incorrectly expect our schools to provide our children, but schools can't or won't do it. Moms and Dads do it best.

There was no greater privilege than to be on Mom's "Worry List." That meant one of her brood was having some significant personal problem, such as loss of employment, severe disappointment, illness, or divorce. Mom would then shower so much caring that you just knew everything would be OK. She would just fuss you back to happiness. Her energy extended over long distances, whether by phone or letter. We always had a concerned and practical friend. She gave her time constantly and her possessions often. One peculiar life-long trait of hers was entering contests hoping to win just a little extra money to give to a child of hers who was temporarily struggling. She entered so many contests that the postage she used would alone be a tidy sum. But you know what? It wasn't the funds we needed. It was her encouragement. All eight of us finished college, and five of us have advanced degrees, and she never did win a give-away contest.

And so, what can we say for the life of Winifred, our mother, our friend? Dad and I had no trouble. We instantly agreed while weeping together that she's already in heaven. She's already praying and caring for us and for you. She's already on a celestial committee organizing God's kingdom. I ask you to consider her as a modern-day hero because we need more like her today. I'll ask you to forgive me for my biased remarks, but I can't think of a more balanced, friendly, ethical, generous, loving person short of Mother Teresa perhaps, but Teresa hasn't brought eight children into the world.

Lastly, I'd ask you to remember our Dad, who had the sense to marry Mom and successfully shared her journey in this world for such a long time. I pray for his health and endurance and commend him for being co-partner in giving me and my brothers and sisters such a wonderful infrastructure in life. I'm also mindful of Mother's extended family and friends who are uniquely fine and uplifting people who also add joy to our lives. Let us say goodbye to the body of Winifred but carry with us the multitude of wonderful memories of her spirit.

THE BOOK OF RON

U.S. military delivering Adam Deger bread to St. Elizabeth Hospital during the 1913 flood

The Begots

I am Ronald Thomas Deger Sr., the second of eight siblings begot by Robert (Bob) and Winifred (Winnie) Grant Deger. I was one of six siblings born at Good Samaritan Hospital in Dayton, OH. Older brother Grant came into this world at St. Elizabeth Hospital, also in Dayton and where Dad had been an intern a few years earlier. Sister Chris was born in Windsor Locks, Connecticut, where Dad was a Flight Surgeon in the Army Air Corps during WWII.

I have always been interested in genealogy and local history. My Mother, Winnie, entered a fairly complete family tree into my baby book. This tree went back five generations. On my paternal side, the family surnames are Deger and Hochwalt. On my maternal side, they are Grant and Briggs.

Subsequent to the entries in my baby book, I have been able to broaden this out a little more. I currently have over 1000 names in my Family Tree Maker program. However, I am greatly lacking the many records a true genealogist would require such as birth, marriage, and death records.

Generation one:
Looking at the Deger side, the earliest entry I have is **Christoph Deeger** (yes, 2 e's). He was born about 1723 in Dertingen, Wertheim, Germany, and died on 9/10/1795 in Helmstadt, Bavaria, Germany. He married **Gertrud**

Schwerthofer. She was born on 7/19/1743 in Helmstadt and died on 9/23/1795.

Generation two:
They had one child, **Thomas Deger**, born in 1764 in Helmstadt. He married **Catherine Kaufmann**. She was born on 9/30/1764 in Helmstadt. I wonder if they were childhood sweethearts. They were married in 1790? He died on 5/2/1827 and she passed away on 9/7/1834, both in Helmstadt.

Generation three:
Thomas and Catherine also had one child, **Melchior Deger**. He was born on 9/3/1799 in Helmstadt. He died on 11/11/1857. He married **Margareta Brust**, daughter of **Michael Brust** and **Margareta Maria Martin**, on 11/12/1822. She died on 1/9/1854 in Helmstadt.

They had a total of 10 children, the fourth of whom was **Michael Deger**. He was born on 2/15/1831 in Helmstadt. He died on 6/14/1892 in Dayton, Ohio, USA.

Michael and Katherine Deger circa 1875

Generation four:
Michael Deger came to the United States around 1850. He came in through the port of Baltimore and traveled to Martinsburg, W.Va. He married **Catherine Sell,** daughter of **John Sell,** about 1855 in Martinsburg. She was born on 1/9/1834 in Hummelberg, Bavaria, Germany. She died on 10/22/1912 in Dayton, OH.

The family moved to St Louis, MO, in 1860 where Michael joined the Missouri Second Infantry Regiment during the Civil War. The Regiment traveled extensively, going to Kentucky, Ohio, Tennessee, Mississippi, then fought at Chickamauga and Missionary Ridge. He was a baker in the Army. He held the rank of Sergeant.

Michael Deger home, Martinsburg W. Virginia - 1850

After the war the family moved again, this time to Dayton, OH. They had five children. The first three were born in W. VA and the last two in Dayton. Teresa (1856-1894), Joseph (1857-1913), John Jacob (1858-1940) were born in W. VA, and Adam (1867-1931) and Christine Catherine (1868 -?) were both born in Dayton.

Michael Deger Bakery, Brown St. Dayton, Ohio, circa 1875

Michael ran a bakery on Brown Street near the University of Dayton. I have a picture of U.S. servicemen delivering bread in a boat from the Deger Bakery to St. Elizabeth Hospital during the great Dayton Flood in 1913. I also have pictures of the family home in W. Va. and the Deger Bakery.

By the way, the reaction to the flood by the citizens, civic and business leaders of Dayton is a real point of pride to me as native of Dayton.

John Patterson was the owner of NCR (National Cash Register company). On Sunday, March 25, 1913, the" Great Rain" started. (My father, Robert J. Deger, had been born on February 23, 1913 in his grandparent's home at Salem and Riverview Avenues right next to the Great Miami River.

It was then that John H. Patterson rose to the greatest moment of his life. It rained all day Sunday and all day Monday. On Tuesday, when he reached the factory at 6:30 AM, he was worried. He went to the roof of the office building and looked over the area. He called for his car and rode about Dayton and up and down the riverbanks. He returned to his office and summoned all of his executives. He quickly sketched out a pyramid organization of the executives to take care of Dayton when the flood came. He then declared NCR out of commission and The Citizens Relief Association came into existence.

All of his resources, organization, and operational skills went into the flood days. He turned his large NCR into a vast relief organization. He took charge of the city and opened his factory to feed, house, clothe, and take care of the sick and injured. He instructed his factory staff to build boats and sent his workers out in those boats to rescue stranded residents. When the officers of the Federal Government reached Dayton, they could only say to him: "We can do nothing more than you have already done."

After the flood receded, his company helped with cleaning up Dayton. He also started a committee to work on preventing such a flood in the future. In about six weeks, the committee raised a fund of 2 million dollars to study the flow of the three rivers and two major creeks that joined together in the Dayton area. (I think our ancestor Coelestine Schwind and his son-in-law, Thomas Hochwalt, owners of the Schwind Brewing Co., were significant contributors to this fund.) Patterson hired Arthur Morgan and his Tennessee-based engineering company to devise a plan to prevent further flooding. They came up with a plan. Out of this came the great engineering work of the Miami Conservancy District. This was a major engineering effort that resulted in the completion of five unique dams and levees throughout the region. It was the largest construction project in the country at that time, around 40 million dollars, and was entirely paid for by **private funding**!!! The dams are unique in that they consist of a large holding area behind the dam. The engineers created a hole in the center of the dam that was designed to allow only the amount of water through it that could be handled by the downstream portion of the river. Everything else backed up behind the dam. There are no gates or moving parts. It is completely unmanned.

Morgan went on to be the President of Antioch College near Dayton and later ran the TVA project for FDR.

Working with Patterson was another NCR Executive, Colonel Edward Deeds. Deeds assisted in the fund-raising and personally ran the Conservancy District. He and Charles Kettering invented the self-starter for the automobile and started a company named Dayton Engineering Laboratories Co. (Delco). They contributed the funds to build the Conservancy District's Headquarters building in downtown Dayton overlooking the Great Miami River where the flooding started in 1913.

Compare this effort to the bumbling efforts of state and federal officials to save New Orleans during Hurricane Katrina!

Compliments of
JOHN J. DEGER
Staple and Fancy Groceries
Both Phones
5th and Howard
DAYTON, OHIO.

Advertisement for the John Deger Grocery - 1908

Back to Michael and Catherine: After Michael died, Catherine ran the bakery for several years.

John & Elizabeth Deger grocery store on Howard St.
Dayton, Ohio - 1910

Generation five:
Michael and Catherine had five children.

Teresa Deger was born in 1856 in W. Va. and died 7/25/1894 in Dayton. She married **Joseph F. Reedley** on 11/23/1873 in Dayton, Ohio.

Joseph Jacob Deger was born on May 22, 1857, in W. Va. and died 7/5/13 in Dayton. He married **Adelaide M Feldmann** in 1880 in Dayton and he later married Margaretta Holzormann on 1/31/1900.

John Jacob Deger was born on 1/9/1858 in W. Va. He died on 4/7/1940 in Dayton. He married **Elizabeth**

Adam Deger Bakery - 1890

Linneman. She was born May 2, 1852, in Louisville, KY. She died on June 22, 1944, in Dayton.

Adam Deger - also a baker - 1890

Adam Deger was born on October 17, 1867, in Dayton. He died on February 16, 1931. He married **Mary Jaekle**, daughter of Charles Jaekle and Bernadina Washmuth on September 24, 1890, in Emmanuel Church in Dayton. She was born on October 1, 1867, in Dayton. She died on June 22, 1944, in Dayton.

Christine Catherine Deger was born on December 12, 1868. She married **Edward Durst**

Generation six:
John Jacob Deger and Elizabeth Linneman had three children:

Urban Adam Deger was born on October 15, 1885, in Dayton. He died on August 4, 1962, in Dayton. He married **Agnes Louise Hochwalt,** daughter of Edward Andrew Hochwalt and Emma Teresa Schwind, on June 15, 1909 in Dayton. She was born on April 8,

Urban Deger in front of door with his mother Elizabeth and sister Leila to the left and sister Viola, an unidentified woman, and his father John to his right

1887, in Dayton. She died on July 10, 1974, in Dayton.

Leila Deger was born on August 17, 1887, and died on August 19, 1963, in Dayton. Leila was never married.

Viola Deger was born on October 14, 1889. She married **Edward Hanbuch.**

Generation seven:

Urban and Agnes Deger had two living children.

Thomas Edward Deger was born on September 4, 1911. He died on July 13, 2007. He died in Lansdale, Montgomery County, Pennsylvania. According to my records, he was the longest lived (95+) Deger that I know of. He married **Eleanor Gordon Evans** on June 29, 1935. She was born on June 26, 1913. She died on March 17, 1959. He then married **Frances Clare McAdoo** in 1960. She was born on April 26, 1921. She died on February 25, 1978. The children of our Uncle Tom and Aunt Eleanor were our first cousins, Mary Ann, Carole, Erica, Steve, Alan, and Nicholas.

Robert John Deger was born on February 23, 1913, in Dayton. He died on October 10, 1998, in Trotwood, Ohio (Maria Joseph Retirement Center, where he had been on the medical staff for over 50 years.) He married **Winifred Ann Grant,** the daughter of Joseph William Grant and Vera Winifred Briggs, on November 5, 1938, in Alma Michigan. She was born on August 15, 1916, in Royal Oak, Michigan. She died on February 5, 1992 in Dayton.

Generation 8:

Robert and Winifred Deger had eight children.

Grant Edward Deger was born on September 15, 1939, in Dayton. He married Peggy Elizabeth Barga on April 16, 1966, in Versailles, Ohio. She was born on December 13, 1941, in

Versailles. He later married **Candice Naomi Zehnder**, daughter of Fred and Ruth Zehnder, on August 6, 1988, in Bellingham, Washington. She was born on December 30, 1946.

Ronald Thomas Deger was born on May 21, 1941, in Dayton. He married **Joyce Josephine Niekamp**, daughter of Albert P. Niekamp and Florentina Matilda Link, on May 30, 1964, in St. Sebastian Church, Mercer County, Ohio. She was born on June 15, 1941, in Mercer County (at home).

Robert John Deger Jr. was born on June 7, 1943, in Dayton. He married **Barbara Munich** on July 14, 1979, in Hillsboro, Ohio. She was born on March 9, 1952.

Christine Louise Deger was born on August 1, 1945, in Hartford, Conn. She married **John "Jack" O'Brien** on June 15, 1968, in Corpus Christi Church, Dayton. Jack was born on May 16, 1938.

Paula Ann Deger was born on August 1, 1948 (same birthday as Chris) in Dayton. She died on January 3, 2007, in Spokane, WA. She married **Robert Lawrence "Robin" Cooper Jr.** on June 12, 1976, in Denver CO. He was born on May 29, 1951.

Elizabeth Clare Deger was born on June 30, 1950, in Dayton.

Philip Joseph Deger was born on November 4, 1955. He married **Kathy Brunet** on June 14, 1980, and they had two daughters: Molly (10/12/80 and Beth (2/23/82). He later married Terri Nevius Sacksteder, who was born on 5/25/49.Terri had three daughters by a previous marriage, Lori (5/4/75), Kristi (4/24/79), and Julie (9/7/80).

Douglas William Deger was born on 4/30/1957.

My mother, Winifred Ann Grant Deger, descended from the Grant lineage on her paternal side and the Briggs family on her maternal side. Any missing dates are the fault of the author, who could not locate definitive data.

Generation one

Thomas Grant was born in County Durham, Yorkshire, England late in 1764, and died in Marion County, Ohio May 2, 1823. He married **Mary Powell**, also from Yorkshire. She died in 1837 in Marion County, Ohio. They had eight children: **Mary, Margaret, Sarah, Thomas Jr., Jane, Ellen, Hannah,** and **William**.

Generation two

William Grant was born 12/11/1811 in Appelton, Roebuck, Yorkshire, England and died in 1894 in Springfield, Ohio. William Grant founded a meat market in 1834 in Springfield, Ohio. It closed 98 years later in 1932 under the direction of Irving Grant. It had operated under several names including Grant's Meat Market and William H. Grant & Sons Meat Market.

William married **Nancy McConnel** a native of Columbus, Ohio. The children of William Grant and Nancy McConnel were: **Martin N., Thomas P., Mary J. Grant Mulholland, Fannie Grant Petts,** and **William Henry**.

Our busy patriarch William Grant later married **Nancy McCormick** who was born on 5/24/1814 in Chillicothe, Ohio. Their union gave us **Martin, Lavinia, Fannie,** and **Mary**. Nancy McCormick died 12/11/1850.

William married once again to **Martha Lee Darling** on 4/29/1852. Their children were **George** born 1855 and died 1934, and **Harrie**t born 1860 and died 1941.

Generation three
William Henry Grant was born on 6/5/1836 in Springfield, Ohio. He died 2/3/1912 at 321 N. Plum St. Springfield, Ohio. He married **Lucy Read Garner** on 11/23/1865 in Piqua, Ohio, daughter of John Garner and Elizabeth Esterbrook Read. Lucy was born on 11/10/1841 in Piqua, Ohio and died 8/1/1917 in Springfield.

The children of William Henry and Lucy Grant were: **Bessie Fowler**, born 1/17/1867, **Edward Crum**, born 1/3/1868 in Springfield, Ohio, married 10/13/1891, and died 6/22/1927, **Harry Garner**, born 8/2/1870, married 6/22/1908 in Trinity Episcopal Church Chicago, Illinois where our distant and meritorious relative ZeBarney Phillps Jr. was pastor (see page 19), and died 12/13/1943, **Nellie Fowler**, born 12/19/1872 and died 7/23/1945, **Howard Hayes**, born 9/17/1876 in Springfield, Ohio, married in 9/24/1901 and died 2/22/1962, and **Abbie Whitcomb**, born 5/4/1882 in Springfield, Ohio, married 10/11/1904 and died 2/18/1976.

Generation four
Edward Crum Grant was born 1/3/1868 in Springfield, Ohio. He married **Daisy Phillips** 10/13/1891, daughter of ZeBarney Phillips Sr. and Sallie Essex Sharp. Daisy was born 10/16/1867 in Springfield, Ohio, and died in Chicago, Illinois in 1908. Their children were: **Joseph William Grant**, born 8/25/1891 in Springfield, Ohio and died 7/17/1951 in Lansing, Michigan, **Edward Phillips**, born 6/3/1893 in Springfield, Ohio, and died 12/22/1900, **Sallie Essex** born 3/1/1896 in Portsmouth, Ohio, and **Blanche Carter**, born 11/3/1904 in Chicago, Illinois and died about 1932 in Connecticut.

Generation five

Joseph William Grant our maternal grandfather (see page 11), was born 8/25/1891 in Springfield, Ohio and married **Vera Winifred Briggs** our maternal grandmother (see page 12) on 2/21/1911 in Newport, Campbell County, Kentucky. She was the daughter of Rufus Briggs and Mary Josephine Irons. Mary was born on 3/9/1891 in Austin, Union Township, Ross County, Ohio. She died 2/11/1969 in Springfield, Ohio.

The children of Joseph and Vera Grant were: **Joseph William Jr.**, born 6/14/1913 and died 1/1972 in Brookfield, Connecticut, **Winifred Ann** our mother, born 8/16/1916 in Royal Oak, Michigan, married our father Robert 11/5/1938, Alma, Michigan, and died 2/5/1992 in Dayton Ohio, and **Phyllis,** born 4/20/1919 and died 8/22/02 in Huntsville, Alabama.

Joseph William Jr. married **Valfred F. Langlie** in California. Their children, our first cousins, are **Joseph W. III** born 8/9/1952, **Cindy** born 9/20/1954, and **Jeff** born 2/15/1957.

The eight children of Winifred Ann and Robert J. Deger are the "Great Eight" about whom this book is written.

The children of Phyllis and Don Maliskey and our first cousins are **Don "Kim"** born 10/1/42 in Macron, Georgia and died 2/19/04, **John** born 5/15/48 in Fort Knox, Kentucky, **Thomas** born 9/16/49 in Yokohama, Japan, and **Wally** born 7/11/56 in Frankfurt, Germany.

The following history of the Briggs family is the record of our mother's maternal lineage.

Generation one

Joseph Briggs was born about 1746 in Virginia. He died in 1808 in Pendleton county Virginia (now West Virginia). He married **Rosanna ?** about 1762. She was born about 1747 in Virginia and died about 1800 in Pendleton County, Virginia (now West Virginia. Apparently their only child was **Joseph Briggs, Jr.**

Generation two

Joseph Briggs Jr. was born 2/28/1773 in Pendleton County, Virginia (now West Virginia) and died 7/21/1828. He married **Catherine Harper** in 1794, the daughter of Adam Harper and Christina. She was born in 1774 in the same Pendleton County, and died 9/16/1846 in Frankfort, Ross County, Ohio. Their solitary child was **Charles Briggs**.

Generation three

Charles Briggs was born 6/23/1803 in Austin, Concord Township, Ross County, Ohio. He died 5/30/1879 in Austin. He married **Catherine Mallow** 11/29/1829. (See page 90 to learn the amazing link of the Mallow family to the first Caucasian of European descent to have been born in Ohio territory). Catherine was the daughter of Adam Mallow and Phoebe Dice. She was born on 4/3/1811 in Austin, Ohio. She died 5/9/1888 in Austin, Ohio.

The children of Charles and Catherine were: Amanda, born 1831 in Ross County, Ohio and died 11/25/1892, **Allison**, born 10/20/1833 and died 3/30/1891 in Concord Township, Ross County, Ohio, **Martin**, born 10/30/1836 and died 9/7/1868, **Joseph**, born 12/29/1842, **Rufus W.**, born 2/22/1850 in

Austin, Ross County, Ohio, and died 11/1901, and **Charles G.** born 6/8/1856.

Generation four
Red-haired **Rufus Washington Briggs** was born 2/22/1850 in Austin, Ross County Ohio. He died 11/1901. He married **Mary Josephine Irons** on 12/24/1879 in Pike County Ohio. She was the daughter of Joseph Irons and Samantha Wilcox and was born 1855 in Beaverton, Pennsylvania. She passed in 1941.

The children of Rufus and Mary were: **Chloe** ("Bessie), "**Mazie**", **Catherine** ("Katie"), **Janet** ("Nettie"), **Grace** born 12/12/1889 and died 10/18/1945, **Vera Winifred** born 3/9/1891 and died 2/11/1969, and **Willa Rufena**, born 9/23/1894 and died 8/11/1972.

Generation five
Generation five is all about **Vera Winifred Grant** who gave life to our mother. But I wish to include her 6 other sisters because they were of happy memory. (The Author, Grant Deger)

Chloe "Bessie"Briggs married George Lafferty and their son was **William Briggs Lafferty** born 1910 and died 1988 in Springfield, Ohio.

Mazie Briggs lived to a ripe old age. I remember her for her fantastic cherry pies.

Catherine ("Katie") Briggs married Harry Chapman who was born 5/24/1877 in Chatteris, England and he died 1937 in Royal Oak, Michigan.

Janet ("Nettie) Briggs died in St. Petersburg, Florida.

Grace Briggs was born 12/12/1889 and died 10/18/1945 in Haslett, Michigan.

Vera Winifred Briggs, was born 3/9/1891 in Austin, Union Township, Ross County, Ohio. She died on 2/11/1969 in Springfield, Ohio. She married **Joseph William Grant** on 2/21/1911 in Newport, Campbell county, Kentucky. Our grandfather Joe Grant died on 7/17/1951 in Lansing, Michigan. He was an Accountant for the Oldsmobile Division of General motors. He had a heart attack and died at his desk.

The children of Vera and Joseph Grant were **Joseph W.**, **Winifred Ann** (our mother) and **Phyllis.**

Willa Rufena Briggs, was born 9/23/1894 in Royal Oaks, Michigan and died on 8/15/1972 in Tucson, Arizona. (See page 166 for my sister Beth's happy memories of Aunt Willa playing Santa Claus). She married Charles Pierce Ackert on 5/12/1920 in Royal Oaks, Michigan. He was born in Little Rock, Arkansas. He died in Tucson, Arizona. Willa and Charles Ackert gave birth to Charles Briggs Ackert who was born 12/11/1930 and married Pat in Tucson where he still lives.

Our first home: Dad's medical office was on the first floor, and his family lived upstairs – early 1940s

The "Peach"

Somewhere in my youth, my mother nicknamed me the "Peach." I am not sure how this started. We had a peach tree in our back yard of my second home at 617 Kenilworth Ave. That may have been where the idea came from. I am sure the name did not come from Grant and me forcing Rob to run around the peach tree naked. I think the name came from my upbeat personality and being helpful around the house. There is a message from Mom in my Baby Book that might shed further light on the name. April 19, 1944. "Ronnie, darling, I'd like a dozen like you. Always brimming over with laughter – from the minute you get up in the morning. Very affectionate and what's nicest you'll do what you're told. Keep that gift, honey. It's priceless." Whatever, some of my siblings still refer to me as "The Peach."

I was born on May 21, 1941, six and a half months before we entered World War II. My hospital bill from Good Samaritan Hospital totaled $67.37 for 10 days in the hospital, room and board ($5.50/day), delivery room ($6.00), care of baby ($10.00) and so forth. Dad got a discount of 10% for being on the Good Samaritan staff. We were living at 1325 Salem. Dad's office was on the first floor and we lived above the office.

According to my baby book, I was standing alone at 11 months and walked at 12 months. I smiled at three months and then all the time. I washed dishes at age seven and was also cutting grass at age seven.

Dad went into the Army Air Corps on September 16, 1942. Mom and her three boys stayed home while Dad went to various duty stations.

In 1944, the family joined Dad, who was an Army Air Corps Flight Surgeon stationed at Bradley Field in Hartford, Connecticut. We lived in Windsor Locks, Conn., a suburb of Hartford.

I have very few memories of life in Connecticut. Our house was on a hill and I remember a tall wall between our front yard and the sidewalk below. One winter the snow was almost to the top of that wall. I remember a fighter plane crashing into the Connecticut River near our house. I remember running through a corn field in back of our house. I remember a big Thanksgiving dinner at the air base for all hands. I also remember bringing Chrissy home from the hospital after she was born. Mom was holding her in the front seat and I was in the back. I held up my hand and put it up to her small hand. We all laughed about how much bigger my hand was than hers.

In 1945, we moved back to 1325 Salem Ave. over Dad's office and took over one room on the first floor for an extra bedroom. There were now four kids in the family. We lived there for the next three years. During that time, we got a pet collie name Lassie. The name was pretty original, don't you think? Poor Lassie did not last too long and met an untimely demise on busy Salem Ave.

At age five, I contracted a very serious case of measles, which had a very bad effect on my right eardrum. During my early years I also got many of the childhood diseases like croup, chicken pox, and mumps,

I had the privilege of attending a fairly elite kindergarten named Mrs. Hoffman's Private School on North Robert Blvd. in downtown Dayton. Mrs. Hoffman picked me up in her car and returned me to home after school. There were a number of other kids in the car. The problem was that I got carsick with some regularity. If I were her, I would have insisted my parents find another mode of transport to the school. She did not do this and just cleaned up me and my messes. God bless the patient Mrs. Hoffman.

One event at the school was an Easter Parade. Mom saved a full-page article from the Dayton Daily News dated April 5, 1947, which shows the picture of seven little boys and seven little girls holding hands walking down a sidewalk while dressed in our finest Easter clothes. All of the girls were wearing their Easter bonnets. The boys were wearing suits with short pants.

I got my first trip to the Good Samaritan Hospital Emergency Room. Grant and I were playing in the back yard when for some reason Grant decided to shove me to the ground. I fell against the root system of a big old tree and broke my collarbone.

Grant had a friend Norman Gunn (commonly referred to as "Son of a Gunn"). It was at the Gunn's home that I watched TV for the first time. I remember watching Milton Berle on the Texaco Star Theatre. He was a funny slapstick comedian and he made us laugh.

It was on Salem Ave. that I first helped in the kitchen, helping Mom mixing cookie dough and fighting to lick the spoon. I also helped out with a little cooking. Mom also took us to the neighborhood library almost every Saturday morning when we lived on Salem Ave. She was an avid reader, often checking out five or six books at a time. The kids would stay for the story hour at the library. I really liked the library. It was built in the English Tudor style. It had the most wonderful smell to it. It was full of interesting books. This early exposure to the world of books was very helpful in our later quest for education. This library was consolidated with a new library and closed in 2016.

Grade School

I started first grade at Corpus Christi School in September, 1947. Dad often drove us to school. Occasionally, we walked or took the public bus. Walking was a chore. My guess was that we were about one and a half miles from school. One time I walked after school with my friend Jack Martin to his house on Cambridge Ave. west of Salem Ave. We played at his house and then I had to walk by myself about a mile up Salem Ave. to my house. Getting to school on a public bus was a challenge. We got the bus across the street from our house. Bus fare was $.03 to downtown and another $.01 for a transfer. We got off downtown and changed busses to get to

Corpus Christi School, which was also on the bus line. Several times I made this trip alone at age six!

Every day before the start of school, the students would line up by classroom in the parking lot. The school had a loudspeaker on the building and the principal would play famous marches like Stars and Stripes Forever and The Washington Post arch. We would then all march from the back to the front of the school in a 2 x 2 formation by classroom starting with the first graders.

On Good Friday, 1948, when Mom was pregnant with Paula, we moved to 617 Kenilworth Ave. On moving day, my parents must have told Grant and me to get lost and stay out of the way. Anyway, Grant and I went to the house of a friend of his, Bob Homewood. From there we went exploring, ending up behind the Tropics Restaurant. The Tropics had a big dirt hill behind it that must have been about 20 feet high and with a pretty steep slope. We played on that hill for a couple of hours even in the rain on Good Friday afternoon. Of course, we were filthy when we got to our new house.

Our new neighborhood was awash with kids most of whom were Catholics going to Corpus Christi Grade School. Across the street were the Klostermans with 9 kids. Jerry K was one of my lifelong friends. Behind them were the Reilings. Dick was one of my best friends and his brother Walt was one of Grant's best lifelong friends. Up the street were the Dahms with 9 or 10 kids. It was a great neighborhood.

While in the second grade, I made my First Communion at Corpus Christi Church. I remember lining up in the cafeteria in the school basement next to the church. At that time, to receive communion you could eat or drink nothing from midnight the night before. There was a drinking fountain in the cafeteria and all I could do was look at it and think of how thirsty I was. We marched 2 x 2 out of the school to Homewood Ave. turning right on Homewood and then right on Forest Ave. to the church. The girls led the parade in their angelic white dresses followed by the boys in their blue suites. Afterwards we went with Grandma and Grandpa Deger and my family for breakfast at the Van Cleve Hotel in downtown Dayton. This was a real treat and Grandpa picked up the tab. I later learned that he sent the same amount as the breakfast tab to Uncle Tom in Pennsylvania to keep things even between his two sons. My teacher, Sr. Delores Marie was a very nice lady and I learned a lot that year.

My third-grade teacher was Ms. Ann Landers, who was caring for her elderly mother. We used to call her "Radio Ears," because she was always telling us not to talk in class because she had ears like a radio and could hear everything we said. At the time, I never questioned whether radios could hear or not. She later became a nun.

In the fourth grade I joined the Cub Scouts. Mom and her good friend Dottie Reiling were two of my Den Mothers. I remember making a knight's armor and a helmet using cardboard covered with aluminum foil. We also had our Pinewood Derby races, where we started with a block of wood and formed it into a race car. We would then race against each other in our den. The winners would then race others in our pack (school). From there, the winners would race winners from other packs in the Dayton area.

I had a lot of fun in the Cub Scouts. I developed solid friendships with my fellow scouts, which survive through today. We learned about working together to complete a task or craft.

I remember being very competitive in the classroom. This was particularly true in arithmetic, where I was always racing to beat Bob Musselman in solving math problems.

The Korean War started in June, 1950. Shortly thereafter, they introduced war cards. Just like baseball cards, we could trade cards featuring tanks, Jeeps, F-86 jets, the commander Gen. Douglas MacArthur, and various campaigns. This was an interesting way for someone to make money off of the war.

In the winter of 1950, I was standing in the lunch line in the basement cafeteria at Corpus Christi. I was behind Tom Kuhn, who was wearing a knit hat. As a joke, I pulled off his hat and hit him over the head. What I did not know was that he had a steel boulder in the cap. I caused a bloody mess. When I got home that afternoon, my Mom asked me what I was trying to do. Mrs. Kuhn had called her and must have read the riot act to her. About 40 years later, Jerry Klosterman, Tom Kuhn's cousin, died. At his funeral I saw Tom Kuhn's sister, Jackie. I said hi to her and she suggested I see her mother, as she would recognize me. She sure did. I said hi to Mrs. Kuhn and she immediately said, "oh, you are the guy who hit Tommy over the head!" Several years later, Mrs. Klosterman died, and I went to her funeral. At the reception, I saw Mrs. Kuhn sitting at a table with some friends. I went up to her and knelt down and asked her to forgive me for what I had done probably 45 years before. As an aside, Tom went on to become a priest and eventually was the pastor of my church, The Church of the Incarnation in Centerville. OH. This is the largest parish in the Diocese of Cincinnati. He next went to our current parish, St. Henry. While there he was investigated for being a little too close to a number of altar boys. He later got defrocked and now lives in Cincinnati. I wonder if my blow to the head in the fourth grade had any impact on him.

I dreaded going into the fifth grade. Like all of the other grades, there were two classes of fifth graders. The two nuns that ran the two classes were fairly large, mean-looking ladies that had reputations for being very tough. Their names were Sr. Anna Marie and Sr. Mary Raymond. I was placed in Sr. Anna Marie's class. She was pretty tough and did not spare the ruler to the hand as punishment. Even with all of my fears, I survived.

The fifth grade was when the boys were allowed to play on the side of the hill next to Five Oaks Park. This got us out of the parking lot where the little kids played. We spent most of our time running up and down the hill. Several got hurt running through the little hill made by cinders from the school boiler. They would trip and get cut by the cinders. We did have to be wary of raids from the upper classes. They would swoop down and capture one of us and take him up to their part of the hill and harass him.

In the sixth grade, I had Sr. Constance. She was a little bitty thing. I can still see her pulling on Tom Metzger's sleeve to get his attention. Tom was a pretty big kid and he said he did not feel her pulling on his sleeve.

It was in this class that I got my first and only failing grade. I got an F in conduct. I do not remember what I did but I still remember the F.

I cannot remember my seventh-grade teachers, but I think I had a nun to start and then had two lay teachers to finish up. The male teacher took a number of us by bus to St. Henry, OH, where we were met by a seminarian from the Carthagena Seminary. This was the major seminary for the Precious Blood priests. The assistant priests at Corpus Christi were members of the Precious Blood order. This trip was a blatant recruiting trip. In my day, many young men started in seminaries after the eighth grade. We were given the tour and fed well that day. This seminary was also the site of several "servers' recognition picnics." Little did I know that my future bride Joyce lived on a farm just a few miles down the road.

Our playground this year was most of the way up the hill.

In the seventh grade, we had our first kissing parties where we played "spin the milk bottle."

Eighth grade made us the kings of the hill, as we had the top part. During snowy days we would throw snow balls at the Julienne girls walking to school on Old Orchard Dr. The top also had baseball diamonds and some park playground equipment. We had a good time up there.

My teacher was Sr. Francis Beatrice ("Old Franny B"). She was also the principal. She was a great lady and I learned a lot.

At the eighth-grade graduation, Dick Reiling and I were Masters of Ceremony. I was pretty nervous to be speaking in front of our pastor, Msgr. Harry J. Ansbury, the dean of the Dayton Deanery, and all of our teachers, classmates, and parents. I think Dick and I did a fairly good job that day.

Dick and I also achieved the Boy Scout "Ad Alteri Dei" award. This is the highest scout honor for Catholic Boy Scouts. Boy Scouts were a lot of fun. We did a lot of camping at Cricket Holler campground. I remember our first Scout Master, Barney Barhorst. Barney was a mailman, so he was a good walker. At a retreat campout, we were reflecting on life and Barney had just turned 50. He was sitting on a big tree stump smoking his pipe and noting to us 10- to 13-year-old kids that he was reaching the end of his life. He advised us to live a good life in order to be prepared to meet our maker. This was a pretty heady topic for his young audience.

Our second Scout Master was George Schour (pronounced Shower). He was a pretty young guy who lived in an apartment one block behind our house. He named his first child "April." I remember one meeting where he introduced us to boxing. I had to fight my friend Dick Reiling, and we agreed to take it easy on one another. A few weeks later, Walt Reiling and Grant egged Dick and me to repeat that fight in the Dineen's back yard. It was snowy, and the ground was frozen. We went at it pretty hard, with Grant and Walt yelling at us. Dick and I got madder and madder at each other. The fight made its way into the frozen alley. Before I knew it, Dick was on top of me pounding my head into the frozen concrete. At that point our elder brothers broke up the fight.

Kissing parties continued in the eighth grade. At one party, Carol Keneer's mother held the flashlight for her daughter Carol when we played flashlight. This game was played in a dark room. All of the couples were kissing. If someone was caught not kissing, they were out. If a girl was holding the flashlight, she would trade places with the girl that got caught. It was a good socializer.

While at Corpus Christi, we got a number of field trips. I mentioned the altar servers' party at Carthagena. The servers also went to LeSourdesville Lake, which was an amusement park. The traffic boys made several train trips to see the Cincinnati Reds at Crosley Field, a short walk from the train station. Traffic boys were older classmates trained to use a flag to hold traffic where the children crossed.

During my grade school years, we went to a number of camps. I already mentioned the campouts at Cricket Holler while in the Boy Scouts. I also went a couple of years to Fort Scott Camp on the northwest side of Cincinnati. This was a two-week camp, and I got a little homesick during the two-week duration. It was later closed, as it was next door to a Super Fund nuclear processing site.

The YMCA in downtown Dayton also ran a number of day camps at Sinclair Park, which I thought was a gigantic forest off Shoup Mill Road. It turned out that it was only 18 acres, but it was fairly wooded and had a big ravine running through it. We would play games like Capture the Flag. Two teams would establish a secret base camp for their flag. The objective was to find and capture the other team's flag and get it successfully back to your base. We sang songs going to and coming from the camp.

Newsboy

I started delivering papers at nine. My first route was for the old Dayton Press. This was an advertising paper that was pretty much delivered to every house on my route. I had about 200 customers that were delivered once a week. We had to collect for this paper, and the charge was $0.10/month. Many people objected to paying because it was mostly ads. A year or so later I got a Dayton Daily News route. I had about 50 customers to whom I delivered six afternoons a week and the much heavier Sunday morning edition. I was at the same branch with Grant. Grant had been named an "Honor Newsboy" and was awarded a green bag for carrying papers. His green bag really stuck out against most of the rest of us carrying a dirty gray bag. Anyhow, his award put a lot of pressure on me to also become an "Honor Newsboy," which I did the next year. My first route was on Main Street and then up Santa Clara Ave.

My second route covered one half of a block on Victor Ave. It started with two 4-family apartments followed by a couple of 12-family apartments. I would then cross Victor Ave. to an 8-family apartment, followed by a few houses. One of the houses presented a real challenge to throw a paper from the sidewalk onto their porch. The porch was covered with a canvas awning and had a brick wall in front of it about three to four feet high. This left about a four-foot opening. Add a couple of vases on the brick wall and it became a challenge to throw a newspaper from the sidewalk onto the porch while riding a bike. After a little practice, I could do it every time. The route concluded with a 26-unit apartment. There were 12 apartments on each of the three floors. All I had to do was stand in the middle of each floor and throw a paper in front of each of my customer's doorways. It was very easy to do. If I hustled, I could complete my route in six minutes. My total time from the time I left my house, bicycled to the paper branch, folded and/or stuffed advertising inserts into my papers, delivered the papers, and then returned home was only about 45 minutes.

In the eighth grade I got a Journal Herald route. This paper was printed six days a week in the morning. I would get up around 4 AM and pick up my papers in front of a drug store. I then proceeded to Fountain Ave., where I delivered around 60 papers. My route consisted of mostly houses with a few 4-family apartments. I would get home around 5-5:30 AM and go back to bed until 6:45 AM. This left me free for after-school football, baseball, and basketball practice.

I was not a good baseball player because I could not hit very well. I was decent in basketball and was one of two seventh graders to make the CYO team. Football was a disaster. My team had three different coaches. I played nine different positions that year, skipping only quarterback and center. We did not score one point all year! One game our end caught a long pass 15 feet behind the opponents. He was clearly free to score, but he tripped on the twenty-yard line. That same game we were first and goal on the one-yard line. We ran three plays and then fumbled before going in. Most of the games ended with us losing around 50 to 0. We finally got a new coach close to the end of the year. He had played semipro ball. The last game was against Shawen Acres Orphanage where we only lost 12-0.

High School

Going to high school was a big deal. Chaminade High School was an all-boys school with around 1200 boys. It was a local powerhouse in football and had won the City Championship ten years in a row. They also had very good baseball and basketball teams. I tried out for basketball, but there were just too many guys with more talent than I had. I did play intramural basketball in my first two years. I was also in the band for two years playing the trombone.

Academically it was divided into Academic (College Prep), Business, and Vocational (Mechanical Arts). As a freshman we were assigned to a classroom alphabetically by our last names. I was in 1B with students whose last name began with a C through F. I finished second in my classroom. The next year they reassigned all of the students into classrooms according to your academic ability. I found myself in Class 2A. That meant I was now in a room with 35 of the brightest sophomores at Chaminade. Needless to say, I was not #2 in that class. I never did understand the logic of this reorganization. I was also in 3A and 4A. At my 50th reunion, several people were still saying "oh you were one of those brains in 4A." Fifty years is a long time to carry a grudge or be jealous.

As freshmen, we were housed in the old Emmanuel Parish School. This was a block and a half from the main campus containing the cafeteria. At lunch we would be marched 2 x2 down Franklin St. We would turn right onto Ludlow Ave. and then enter the senior building. We would proceed to the boys' restroom to wash up, and then again be marched to the cafeteria door. After eating, we would line up in the hall and march back to the restroom. After using the restroom, we again formed up and marched back to Emmanuel School. I wonder if kids today have to do all that marching.

In my freshman year, a friend of mine suggested that I join him in the service club. I thought he said the server's club as in serving Mass. I later found out that the service club did things like wash and wax the cafeteria floor, clean up the gym floor before and after basketball games, usher school plays, and a host of other jobs. In my sophomore and junior years, I also joined the cafeteria squad. This was the dish washing crew. The job paid $0.35 per day. This is the reason I grew 6" and gained 75 pounds in high school. A meal only cost $0.35. With this job, I could double the amount of food that I got for lunch.

I made the Honor Roll in each of the first three years and made the National Honor Society in my senior year. I still delivered newspapers my freshman year. After that, I joined Grant working in a local drug store. My main job was being a soda jerk. I could put together a mean banana split or sundae. Chocolate malts and shakes were another specialty. Cokes, ice cream cones, ice cream sodas, and hand-packed ice cream flowed from my talented hands. We also waited on people buying the general merchandise.

The store was open on Sunday mornings and closed at noon and then reopened at 6 PM. On Sunday afternoon, one of us had to come in and wash and wax the floor and do some general clean up. Our pay was $0.55/hour to start with and later we got some $0.05/ hour annual raises. I supplemented my income throughout high school by cutting grass, raking leaves, and shoveling snow for neighbors or ex-newspaper customers. The owner, Don Hersman, told me he hired Grant and me because we were sons of a doctor who would hopefully send prescription business his way. He said he was a little disappointed because Dad wrote very few prescriptions.

In the summer between my junior and senior years, Dick Reiling, Jerry Schmitz, and I took a two-week trip to Florida. Dick was a civil war buff, so before going to Florida we had to see many of the major battlefields. We saw Harper's Ferry, Gettysburg, Antietam, Fredericksburg, Manassas, Andersonville prison site, Charleston, and others that I now forgot. We then went down the east coast of Florida to Miami and then across the Tamiami Trail and back up the Gulf Coast. It was a ton of fun and took two weeks. During the trip, we blew the head gasket on Mrs. Reiling's 1949 Plymouth Station Wagon twice. It cost us about $150 each time and wasted half of a day each time. A bigger problem was we split the cost of the repairs both times. This was in the days we carried traveler's checks and not credit cards. My part was $100 and took a chunk out of my available funds.

Dick and Jerry made the first bikini sighting while I was asleep on my stomach on the beach. Naturally, they made no attempt to wake me. They saw the girl and I got sunburned. Life is not always fair.

In my junior year, I was elected Treasurer of our Corpus Christi Parish Teen Club. My senior year, I was elected

President. The club met in the Recreation Center at the parish. This building was built during my freshman year. We had a number of club activities. The most fun was when we hosted sock hops for other Catholic parishes in Dayton. They reciprocated and hosted dances at their parishes. This filled our social calendar for the school year with once-a-month dances.

There were also weekly Friday night dances at Club Cayoda in the Loretto building in downtown Dayton. The Loretto was a large residential center for Catholic young ladies that came to Dayton to work after high school. It was run by an order of Catholic nuns. This provided the residents with a safe place to stay. During the dance, I was generally one of those wallflowers too afraid to ask a girl to dance. As I got older, I got a little more confident.

Jobs

During my senior year I began a job at Dayton Nut Products Co. owned by Charles Reiling, Dick's uncle. I was paid the handsome sum of $1.00/hr. I was kind of a jack of all trades. I cooked and packaged nuts, made peanut butter, unloaded truckloads of incoming nuts, and on occasion drove packaged nuts to our Tipp City plant and Cincinnati warehouse. This company sold nuts to various retailers like our drug store and had the exclusive contract with the Winn Dixie Supermarket chain. That was why they also had a warehouse in North Carolina and another plant In Florida.

One day, a truck with a 40-foot trailer pulled into the alley next to the plant. The company had hired two day labors to help me unload the truck containing a very full floor to ceiling load of 100-pound bags of nuts. One of the day labors walked away the minute the driver opened the door. The other quit after he put the first bag on his back. That left yours truly to unload the whole 40,000 lb. load. I had to take them from the alley into the plant, turn left and left again, and stair step stack them against the wall.

Cashews presented another packaging problem. They were packaged 25 lbs. in a metal container. Two of these containers were packaged in a rough sawn wooden box full of splinter opportunities. The driver would unload the boxes using a roller conveyer on the truck floor. The boxes would come off of the truck on a conveyer sloping down from the truck to a lower conveyer about 10 ft. long. I would then unload these boxes onto a skid. If you were not paying attention or were too slow, you could get your fingers crushed between two boxes.

Fun Times

During high school, my buddies and I started playing poker at our various houses. The game could start after a Cayoda dance or on a weekend. These games continued through college and after we were married. They ended after we each had a couple of kids and we could not afford to lose much money.

I was very lucky growing up. Mom and Dad liked to vacation once a year. Usually Dad set it up to take a vacation the first two weeks of August. One time we went with my Godparents Paul and Charlotte Foy and their kids to Brown County State Park in Southern Indiana. This area was the site of two other State Park vacations, Spring Mill and McCormick's Creek State Parks. We also took a trip to Crystal Lake in northeast Indiana, where the wait staff at the Inn sang songs to the guests. One line of one of the songs was "The tips at the Lakeside they say they're very fine, I've been here all summer and haven't got a dime. Gee but I wanna go home."

Another time we went to western Michigan, but I forgot which beach. I know we were near Holland, Michigan, as I bought some wooden shoes there. Also, there was a Kenilworth Ave. neighbor, Charles Danis (my future employer) and his family, and Fr. Beckman, our Assistant Priest at Corpus Christi. All I really remember was getting to the beach and running into the water. It was freezing, and we ran right back out.

Most of the time we went to Indian Lake, which was about a one-hour drive from Dayton. We always had to stop in the DeGraf Creamery in DeGraf, Ohio. We would pile out of the car and into the store where we were each treated to an ice cream cone of our choice.

We rented a waterfront cabin from the same guy every time. The Reilings were in a rented cabin near us. The Foys had their own cabin on Fox Island about a mile across the lake. At first, we rented a row boat to go fishing. Later we had a 16-foot Chris Craft run-a-bout that Dad built in the basement. We named it The Wet Pet. Grant and I helped put in many of the 1000 screws in the boat kit. We cracked the hull during assembly of the bow. We were able to fix it. Our main problem was that it did not fit out the basement door. Dad had to take the door frame apart to get the boat out. We had all of a 7-1/2 HP Elgin outboard motor. The boat could do about 20 mph, which was plenty fast for a kid to drive. We had several years of fun in this boat until a certain brother two years younger than me hit a stump while going through an area where there were a lot of tree stumps under the water. He should not have taken the boat anywhere close to that clearly marked area. This collision knocked the motor off of the boat and into the water. The motor was shot.

Indian Lake had an amusement park. You could drive your boat to the park and leave it in their marina. The Foys had a big Chis Craft Cruiser with a big inboard motor. It rode very smooth with the engine making noise almost like a big Harley Davidson motorcycle. Norman Foy, Paul's brother, would often take us at night to the amusement park in this boat. We were in tall cotton country going to the park in a big Chris Craft.

In 1949 we came very close to a tragedy. We were all sitting around the concrete patio in our back yard near the water. Just then Walt Reiling comes running up from his house two doors away and jumps into the water next to our dock. He came out of the water holding our one-year old Paula, still in her stroller. Somehow, she must have started the stroller rolling and it went into the lake. Nobody saw her but Walt on his dock. Thank God he saw her.

My friend Bob Musselman also had a boat. After he got a car in his junior year of high school, we started boating on the Miami River by Triangle Park. We did a lot of water skiing on the river east of the park. With all of the pollution in the water, I am lucky I did not get polio or some other disease. We would also go with our group to Indian Lake for more skiing. We also stayed overnight and played poker on the boat.

Automotive Adventures

Larry Horvath and I each bought a 1953 Chevrolet for our first cars. He was kind of a nut behind the wheel. I remember him running the car to maximum speeds in first and second gears. He rode his car very hard, and one time he had to repair the engine. I helped him a little getting the engine apart in his garage. The problem came when he went to reassemble the motor. He could not get it all together again. He was out of commission for weeks. I never tried to take mine apart. However, my transmission went out and it cost me about $100 to repair it.

Since I had spent my savings account on buying my car and the cost of insurance, I had to borrow some money from Grant. In my sophomore year in college, I threw the clutch on the car. I went to Grant with a proposition. If he forgave my debt and fixed the clutch, he could have my car.

College

I started working at the UD Research Institute during my freshman year. This again was $1.00/hour work. I worked in the IBM Room running old IBM punch card machines. This included key punch machines, card sorters, tabulators, and interpreting machines. It was a neat job because to get into any class, you had to get a class card that was created by my department. Therefore, we could avoid the lines and preregister each semester by pulling the appropriate class card while working.

We also ran the grade reports. giving us access to our grades ahead of time. The payroll was run in my department, so we could see the salary of the basketball coach and others. I ended up on the night shift working from around 5 PM to 10 PM. If you want to have fun, you might try running several card sorters at the same time. This machine had a pocket where you could insert about a 6" high handful of IBM cards. It also had 12 pockets that the cards could drop into. The cards had holes in some of the 80 columns. If you were sorting numerically, you would sort each column and the sorter would drop the card in the right pocket. Sorting alphabetically required two passes per column. The letter A has two holes, position 12 and position 1. The letter B is a 12 and a 2, C a 12 and a 3, and so forth. The next group uses the 11 plus 1, 11 plus 2, etc. Finally, the last letters are a position 10 plus a 1, 10 plus a 2, etc. In this case, you have to sort twice on each column. First you sort the 10, 11, and 12 numbers, and then sort the 12 cards into 1 through 9. You then sort the 11 cards into 1 through 9 followed by the 10 cards. I have had cards with 50 columns of alphabetic data that had to be sorted. It might take days to sort some of these jobs. Our night shift could out-produce a much larger day shift because we all ran multiple machines with no interruptions.

That year UD was very short on dorm space, so they rented the Gibbons Hotel in downtown Dayton next to the Dayton Daily News. All out-of-town freshman male students had to live there. It was a fiasco and not a good environment for an 18-year-old boy away from home for the first time. The bars around the hotel and the burlesque house three blocks away all did a booming business. The students would drop things out the window into the alley behind the hotel and try to hit Dayton Daily News trucks waiting to get into the inside news dock to load up with newspapers. One guy threw out a wastebasket full of water. I'm glad he missed. UD only did this that one year, as 95% of the residents were on academic probation after the first semester. The next year, they moved the freshman men to an isolated building on the VA Center in West Dayton.

During my freshman year, I signed up for the U.S. Marine Corps Platoon Leaders Class (PLC). This program involved going to two 6-week summer camps at Quantico, VA. One was after my freshman year and one after my junior year. I would then get my commission as a 2nd Lt. after I graduated from UD. I then had a three-year active duty obligation and a three-year reserve obligation. The trip to Quantico after my freshman year was my first plane trip and was on a propeller-driven TWA airplane. I did not ride a jet until two years later.

In my sophomore year I also got a job driving truck for the Dayton Daily News. I had to join the Teamsters Union, but got paid a whopping $2.98 an hour. On holidays we got paid triple time. I worked part-time around two to three weekdays from noon to about 5:30 PM and all Sunday morning from around midnight until 8 AM. For a year or so, I kept my UD job and worked two jobs.

Over the winter, I met the love of my life, Joyce Niekamp, at an ice-skating party sponsored by UD. I like to say she fell for me, but she was in front of me and fell. I then fell for her. The next day I called her and asked her for a date the next weekend, but she was busy. The next I heard from her she was inviting me to the turnabout tag dance. I jumped on the chance to take her. Our first date was to a movie at the old McCook Theater. It was about a sailing ship of some sort. It was about 10:30 PM when we left the movie. At the time I was on an 11 PM curfew by my parents. I called home and talked to Mom to see if I could stay out later. I promised to wash and wax her station wagon if she said yes, which she did.

Why, one might ask, was I, a 19-year college student, on a parental curfew?   One of the problems was I still lived at home. The other was that over the Christmas break, I was at Mark Fettig's house playing with his younger brother's vibrating football game. We were playing one game after another before I realized how late it was. It was around 2 AM and much too late to be calling home. We decided to keep playing. Of all things, at 6 AM we decided to go to Mass at nearby Corpus Christi Church. We sat near my Grandpa Deger, who was playing the organ at that Mass. Afterwards I went home to an angry parental duo. I explained what had happened, that I was playing games with Mark and just lost track of time. Dad doubted my story because he had gone out looking for me around 6:00 AM and my car was not at the Fettig house. It was then that I told them we went to Mass and that Grandpa could vouch for me. That did not matter, and I was put on an 11:00 PM curfew for the next two months.

Meeting Joyce was the best thing that happened to me at UD. She was a cheerleader, and I had to really scramble to get basketball tickets to watch her. The team played in a 5000-capacity arena with the students on one end. This section could maybe seat 1000 students. I had to get up at 5:00 AM to head to UD and wait outside in front of the ticket window to get a seat. In our junior year, the team made it to the semi-finals of the NIT in NYC. Jack Martin and I drove with our dates, Joyce Corwin and Joyce Niekamp, and two other classmates to NYC. We had a great sleepless time exploring NYC and going to the basketball games. The Flyers won the 1962 NIT. This was the first major tournament win for the team. They had been runners up a number of times but never first. At the time, the NIT was more prestigious than the NCAA. It was a very big win.

It was also great to spend the school year with Joyce. She also worked at the UD Research Institute and stayed though the summer. A couple of years we each played softball on a different team in a UD League. When a men's team played Joyce's team, the men had to bat with your non-dominant side. At the end of summer, Joyce always had a higher batting average than me.

We went to all of the dances and many other school activities. One year she and a number of her friends lived in an apartment three blocks from my house. There were two other groups of UD students living in that apartment complex. That year I became the duty driver for all three groups.

Marine Corps and Marriage

I asked Joyce to join us for dinner at our house. My little sisters were very impressed with Ronnie's new and almost only girlfriend. After that, she was a frequent visitor to the Deger household and fit right in. We got engaged during our senior year. We planned a wedding in 1964.

In June 1963 Joyce got her BS degree in Elementary Education and I got mine in Business Management. Joyce went home to teach first grade at St. Henry School in Mercer County, and I went to Quantico, VA, to begin my three-year career with 500 other 2nd Lieutenants at the Marine Corps Basic School. I spent my first year in the Marines as a bachelor in several Marine Corps Schools, and was then transferred to my first duty station, The Marine Corps Supply Center in Philadelphia, PA.

We were married on May 30, 1964, and then got an apartment in Stratford, NJ, across the Delaware River from Philadelphia.

We stayed in Philadelphia for about one year. During that time, we went to the New York World's Fair twice. We also visited several times with my Uncle Tom who lived with his family in Ambler, PA, just north of Philadelphia. It was a good tour and introduced Joyce and me to military life. Joyce got pregnant in January, 1965. Since I was to be transferred in April, the military held up any pre-natal care until we got to our new duty station, Norfolk, VA. Needless to say, we were not very happy campers.

In April, 1965, we moved to Norfolk, where I was assigned to a new duty station. This was as Executive Officer, Marine Detachment, on the USS Wright CC-2, which was one of two capital ships that the US President would ride on if he wanted a command post afloat. We carried a Joint Chief of Staff Group to man the command center. President Johnson spent several days on our sister ship, USS North Hampton, but did not make it aboard our ship while I was there. After spending a year in Philadelphia fighting the "Battle of Broad Street," I was able to spend the next year fighting the "Battle of the Atlantic Ocean."

The Vietnam War started heating up in August, 1965. Since you had to have more than one 1 year to serve and I did not, I was not sent to Vietnam. I was not too upset just a little disappointed. I would have been the first Deger to serve in a war zone since Michael Deger served in the Civil War 100 years before. It was not too long before Brother Rob got that assignment in the U.S. Army.

Ron's Speech to the Chaminade Alumni Panel

April 5, 2011

The Wright Brothers invented the airplane and lived only few miles from here in West Dayton. Wilbur once said that the key to success was to be born in Ohio and pick a good set of parents. He could have added it was even better to be born in Dayton and to pick a good school.

I always felt like I was very lucky. I lived in a good neighborhood; my parents were bright and encouraged learning and love of reading. I came from a large family in a neighborhood full of large families. I am one of eight kids. We never lacked for playmates. My parish was Corpus Christi and they had built a great recreation center that was built when I was a freshman at Chaminade. I was able to spend many hours there playing basketball and volleyball.

Life in Dayton in the 1950s

I went to Chaminade in the 1950s. At that time, we had a great downtown and neighborhoods. The city was growing. In the 1950s, Dayton's population was 275,000 people. We had a number of major employers such as National Cash Register (20,000 jobs), and General Motors Divisions – Delco, Frigidaire, and Inland which had at least 20,000 jobs. Wright Patterson Air Force Base employed around 25,000 people. We had a robust printing industry, which included McCalls (6 million magazines a day), Standard Register, Reynolds & Reynolds, and many others. There were a lot of tool and die shops, foundries, and hundreds of other manufacturing companies.

The city was fairly safe. I took a city transit bus to grade school by myself when I was in the first grade and later to Chaminade. I never had a problem on a bus, and you have never lived until you took a date to a movie in downtown Dayton on a bus.

Chaminade in the 1950s
Chaminade was located downtown and was the only Catholic high school for boys in Dayton. Catholic girls attended Julienne High School. There were 12 public high schools in Dayton at that time.

It was quite a change for me to enter Chaminade. My older brother had already spent two years at Chaminade, so I knew something about the school. However, it was still quite a transition coming to Chaminade.

I had come out of eight years at Corpus Christi school, which had 16 classrooms, all but two taught by Sisters of Charity. We had two lay teachers. Most of the time these teachers were women, but we did have one man for about a month as a substitute.

At Chaminade we had a faculty that was all male and consisted of 24 Marianist priests and brothers and three laymen. The only lady at Chaminade was the principal's secretary, Ms. Agnes Mahle. Having men teachers instead of women was a challenge. Of course, we went to grade school with girls in class. At Chaminade it was all males.

Chaminade enforced discipline by utilizing a demerit system. Coming in late might earn two demerits. Fighting might get you 10 or more demerits. Talking back to a teacher was also a bad deal as far as demerits were concerned. I think it took 15 demerits in a year to get oneself expelled.

We also had a three-book rule. In order to encourage students to study at home, the school had a three- book rule. That meant you had to take at least three3 books home every night. Faculty were stationed at every exit to enforce this rule. Some teachers were stricter than others, so word quickly spread about who was manning each door and students would then go out the exit manned by the less strict teacher.

As a freshman we had to march from the Emmanuel School Building to the Boys Room in the Senior building to wash up. We would then march to the cafeteria. This process was reversed after lunch.

As a sophomore and junior, we went to classes in an old four-story red brick building on the corner of Ludlow and Franklin. This was originally the Notre Dame Academy where my grandmother graduated in 1906 and my Dad graduated in 1930.

It was in this building where I had two of my favorite teachers. Brother Tom Schoen taught me plane geometry in my sophomore year. As a junior, my favorite teacher was my chemistry teacher, Brother Alfred Grisez (we called him Greasy Al, but not to his face). Both of these men made learning their subjects interesting, challenging, and both had a good sense of humor. My favorite senior teacher was Mr. George Early, who also had a great sense of humor.

After my freshman year the school reorganized the students into three groups. The academic group took college preparatory courses, the middle group took some business-related courses, and the last group, called the vocational group, prepared for jobs in industry.

Each homeroom was named with a number and letter. 4A, for example, was the designation of my home room, and the "4" meant you were a senior and the "A" meant you were in the smartest class. 4J were the least intelligent seniors. Whoever devised this method of placing students in homerooms was not dealing from a full deck. Fifty years later at our 50th reunion, I still heard "Oh you were one of those brains in 4A." Even though it was an honor to be in 4A, I did not like my friends thinking I was putting myself on a pedestal. I also felt bad about the other kids having to live daily with the designation of less intelligence. I would have much preferred a more diverse method like we had as freshmen.

For two years I was on the cafeteria squad that washed dishes after lunch. We were paid the princely sum of $0.35

per day. This allowed me the opportunity of buying more food or a dessert at lunch. When I entered Chaminade I was 5' 6" tall and weighed 125 lbs. As a result of good eating, I was 6'2" and weighed 200 lbs. when I graduated.

I was also a member of the service club for two years. A friend asked me to join the service club. I thought that he said the server's club like in serving Mass. Instead I found myself cleaning the gym floor before and after basketball games, scrubbing and waxing the cafeteria floor, and doing numerous clean ups. We also ushered at the school play where Ray Estevez (Martin Sheen) was in the cast.

We all had to wear a tie in those days, and we also had to be neatly dressed. Levi's and T-shirts were not permitted. During my four years at Chaminade, I always wore one of my two knit ties. One was red, and one was black. More than once, the end of my tie dipped into my food at lunch. By the end of my senior year, you could have dipped either necktie in a bowl of water and come up with a decent soup from all the food on it. Notwithstanding the food on the tie, we were fairly neatly dressed and stood out in a crowd of students from other high schools.

Academically Chaminade fared well in standardized tests, debate teams, science fairs, etc. Colleges were very willing to admit Chaminade graduates. Tuition at Chaminade was all of $100 per year ,with $10 of that being paid by your parish.

In sports we did well. Our football team won the school's 14th city championship. In basketball we tied with the class of 1954-55 for the most wins with 17. I did not play varsity sports. There was a lot of competition and it was hard to make the teams. However, we did have a very good intramural program for basketball, and several parishes had high school basketball teams that competed with other parish teams. I played basketball for these latter groups.

Our home football games were played at Welcome Stadium and we always filled up our side. The opponents often filled their side, as Chaminade was the team in everyone's sights. We were the team to beat.

We played most of our home basketball games in our gym. As an aside, we were not allowed to yell or make noises or wave our arms when an opponent was shooting a free throw. It was considered to be unsportsmanlike conduct. The city league passed out a good sportsmanship award every year and we tried to win it.

Socially we also had a good time. An order of nuns ran a large residential center for Catholic young ladies who had come to Dayton to work after high school. It was called the Loretto. Every Friday night during the school year, the nuns hosted a sock hop for Catholic High School kids in the basement of this large commercial building. It was called Club CAYODA. Kids from Chaminade, Julienne, and St. Joseph all came downtown on Friday nights. Many a night I stood around with sweaty palms working up the nerve to ask that beauty across the hall for a dance. Sometimes I succeeded. Other times I ended up talking with some of the other nervous boys.

Chaminade let out at 2:30 in the afternoon. All of the city transit busses going north went through downtown Dayton at Third and Main. Since our students came from all over the area, many had to change busses at Third and Main. Some would just walk around downtown after school. Men of Chaminade stood out. People knew who we were. We had a lot of pride in our school and it showed. I often went to the arcade in downtown, and the merchants respected us as we were a disciplined group. Many of us worked in stores downtown. A Chaminade student was generally a good hire.

Many students who drove cars to school headed straight to St. Joseph or Julienne to meet their girlfriends. The girls' schools let out at 2:45, so you could not delay too long to get there by their dismissal time.

I still feel very lucky to have selected good parents, been born in a good time, in a good city, and to have attended good Catholic local schools from grade school at Corpus Christi, high school at Chaminade, through bachelor's and master's degree levels at The University of Dayton. Chaminade was a tremendous experience. I was also very fortunate in marrying my wife Joyce, as we will celebrate our 46th anniversary in May. We were very fortunate to have three good sons and four darling grandkids. It doesn't get much better.

Addendum

Chaminade Fight Song
Men of Chaminade come fight for your school
Men of Chaminade your colors must rule
If you battle the foe with your courage aglow
All Dayton will know onto victory we will go

Chaminade Anthem
Here's to dear old Chaminade, school of my heart
To thine own self be true, you taught from the start
True to my fellow men
True to my God
True to my Alma Mater Chaminade

STORIES BY ROB, CHRIS, PAULA, BETH, PHIL & DOUG

Rob's Story

When my brother Ron left to serve in the Marine Corps in 1962, I was with Mom when we said goodbye in the driveway of 724 Kenilworth. She was weeping copiously as he drove out of the driveway. In an attempt to comfort her, I told her, "Don't worry, Mom, he'll be alright, and you still have me." At this she burst out into even greater tears.

When I was on orders to Vietnam in the spring of 1968, I had a very poignant and painful meeting with Mom and Dad in Dad's home office one evening. I explained to them that if anything should happen to me, I had this $10,000 GI life insurance of which they were the beneficiaries. Mom burst into extreme tears as I said this. This was very painful for me, because I knew how much she feared the worst.

The morning I left home for Vietnam, I insisted that Mom not accompany me to the driveway because I could not bear a repeat of the scene when Ron left for active duty. We said a tearful goodbye inside the house, then Ron drove me to the airport.

I arrived in Vietnam in May of 1968. My year there was momentous, of course. As an Army intelligence officer, I had a job that was not a combat assignment, but I did face danger regularly. I was assigned to two different jobs, one overt, or open, and one covert, or hidden and top secret.

My overt job was as the Intelligence Officer for the Military Assistance Command Vietnam (MACV) Team Number 37, which involved traveling around Binh Thuan Province to investigate communist Viet Cong activities and troop movements and to analyze their impact in support of the troops of the U.S. 191st Airborne division headquartered in Phan Thiet city, the capital of Binh Thuan. I regularly briefed the commanding officers of the 101st Airborne on my findings. This was the assignment that required that I travel around the province via jeep and helicopter. I often drove in an open jeep alone to various villages in the province subject to Viet Cong ambushes, which were frequent. I was also required to fly to various places regularly by helicopter, which was also high risk. On one occasion, I was on a flight which dropped me off at my home base, and then flew on to another base, where it crashed, killing all on board.

My top secret, covert job was as the Province Area Intelligence Representative (PAIR) for the province. In this capacity, I secretly trained members of the provincial Army of South Vietnam (ARVN) in setting up and operating spy rings in the province to infiltrate and compromise Viet Cong operations.

This was a demanding assignment, but I found it challenging and rewarding. An intriguing aspect of my assignment was that Phan Thiet city was where Ho Chi Minh, the ruthless leader of communist North Vietnam, had briefly taught school as a young man.

In recognition of my work in Binh Thuan Province, I was awarded the Bronze Star medal by the 525th Military Intelligence Battalion in a ceremony at its headquarters in Na Trang city just days before I returned home. Thankfully, I came home in one piece in May of 1969. My joy as the plane left the ground at the Saigon Ton Son Nhut airport is impossible to describe. Let's just say that I felt as if my life was going to be tremendously reinvigorated. I thanked God with deep emotion.

I returned to the USA to Ft. Lewis in San Francisco, then flew to Rochester, Minnesota, to experience a most wonderful time with my brother Grant and his family. Grant even fixed me up for a date with a former Catholic nun who was so recently out of the convent that her hair was still very short. She was a cutie and we had a great time. She was the first date I had had since my R&R in Australia in November of 1968, when I met and dated a beautiful blonde Australian girl I met at the Australian-American Friendship Club my first night in Sydney.

After regaling in Minnesota, I flew onto Dayton to receive a most warm welcome from my family at the airport. Mom and Dad and brothers and sisters greeted me with open arms and much joy!

Rob in uniform back from Viet Nam, visiting his sister Chris

Chris's Story

There are so many wonderful childhood memories that each one of the Deger Eight could write a book of their own. The examples I have written only touch on the joy of life as a Deger.

Growing up with three older brothers was a joy and a challenge. Since I was the oldest of the three Deger daughters, it was up to me to help my brothers realize that girls were different from boys. Unfortunately, I was such a tomboy in my younger years that I am unsure if I was able to impart this information. As a pre-teen, Mother even commented to me on one occasion that she wished I had been the boy, and that sweet Ron (the peach that he was) had been a girl. Hopefully, as I went through puberty and was finished football-style tackling Joe Klosterman (really only one time), Mother was again happy that I was, in fact, her oldest daughter. Of course, by then the family had gratefully added two younger sisters, and we soon became a unit, balancing the gender numbers.

Life at 617 and 724 Kenilworth Avenue was wonderful. My adult friends often complain about my frequent chatter about my happy childhood. Now that I am older, I realize that our parents and the parents of my friends dealt with some pretty serious issues. But during childhood, I felt the world was a wonderful safe place, and we lived without fear. Life with Barb Reiling, Mary Ann Dineen, Roseann Klosterman, Mary Helldoerfer, Chrissy Schneider, Babs Zweisler, and many,

many others was a beautiful thing. We roamed our neighborhood with boom boxes in hand, singing along with the latest hits. Sometimes we ran into a group of guys, and flirted in our naivety, but mostly we talked and laughed and loved our life in upper Dayton View. When younger, we skated with noisy metal-wheeled skates up and down our block, jumped on pogo sticks up to a thousand times without stopping, played jump rope by the hour, flew kites that were tied to the lamp post at night, walked on Dr. Reiling's home-made stilts for miles, and rode our bikes through the stormy pass. Today's world would be ever so much better if kids had the outside opportunities for play that we enjoyed in the 1950s and 1960s.

I loved wearing look-alike dresses with Mom when I was young, remembering with great fondness a green and white-checked gingham dress, worn proudly as a birthday girl of four. At that birthday, celebrated at Indian Lake, I received a little iron and ironing board and a clothes line with little clothes pins along with a doll. I was in heaven. Remembering birthdays, I must share that Paula was born on my birthday, August 1, one year before this celebration. My grandmother, Nana, told me that I was a bear on the day of her birth and cried all day because my mommy was at the hospital and not with me! Nonetheless, I learned to appreciate my little sister. We almost lost Paula on this same family vacation, when she was only one. She was in a baby walker on that day and walked herself down the ramp, in front of the cabin we were renting, descending into the dark water of the lake. Fortunately, Walt Reiling was in the yard of an adjoining Emmelheinz cottage and saw Paula go into the water. Walt dashed into the water and saved Paula's life on the first of her birthdays. Gratefully, the day remained a very good one, celebrated with cake and ice cream. Throughout our childhood Paula and I had wonderful joint birthday celebrations, often with two cakes and two different parties. (After Paula's death at 59, for several years Paula's husband Robin sent me flowers to celebrate our joint birthdays.)

When as a preteen I needed a new dress for some special occasion, Mother took me to Thal's and bought me the most beautiful green and blue silk dress I had ever seen. Even though I was not at my physical best in those years, when I stood under our blooming crab tree for a photo, I thought I was the most beautiful girl in the class in that amazing dress. I know that Dad put mother on a rather stringent weekly budget. However, we all managed to have nice clothes and a pair of new shoes each school year. A shopping trip before school started in the fall included a trip to Rike's fifth-floor tea room. The most beloved meal there was a tasty creamed chicken treat served in a milk glass container created in the shape of a chicken.

I appreciate with great fondness our well-kept baby books. Mother of eight children, our Mom managed to construct the stories of our early lives and kept them alive with pictures and notes in each of our baby books. In my book are cards congratulating my parents at the time of my birth. I also have samples of my hair after early haircuts, height and weight accounts, grade school report cards, lists of what we did and who came to each of my birthday parties, and tracking of our growth and physical, social, and scholastic accomplishments. A real treasure in my baby book is a cartoon drawn by my Dad. He was away in the army for some time when I was very little, so he drew a portrait of me and sent it to Mom. It was not a likeness, but a joy.

I loved having two sisters. We were all so different, but so much alike. By the time I was twelve, there were five boys in the Deger family. The boys were high achievers and we girls needed to stick together to get a "word in edgewise." Beth was quieter as a child. She was a thinker and very sweet. My memories of Paula reveal that she had the most fun. She had many friends and was more willing to go out on a limb. She even got a ticket to see the Beatles in Cincinnati at an early age. I think Beth went to the concert as well. The cost was about $3.50 a ticket at the time. As we grew up, Paula, Beth, and I shared a room. Paula and I had joint library beds and we loved them. They had a sliding door, behind which books and treasures could be stored at the top of the bed. I think Beth's bed was nondescript, but the three in a row beds filled what was meant as the master bedroom. At the time, Beth and I were a little more oriented to cleanliness than was the middle sister. I remember conspiring with Beth to get Paula to do her share of room cleaning on Saturday mornings at 724 Kenilworth Ave. We must have taught her well, as Paula ran a meticulously clean home as an adult.

I sort of enjoy ironing now as an adult, but as a young gal, I hated it. We needed to iron our own blouses before we set off to Corpus Christi and to Julienne in our school uniforms. Because our days were so full of school, play and activities at the Corpus Christi Recreation Center, ironing was usually put off and ended up as a rush job in the early morning before school. It was always a frantic time of day. When able, I remember charging both my little sisters 25 cents for an ironed blouse.

It should be noted that while the three of us girls were close as only sisters can be, we really did not spend much time together. There were so many families in our neighborhood; each of us had several kids close to our own age with whom to play. We tended to spend the majority of our play time with these friends. I do not think we even helped out much around the home. We did have our chores of ironing, cleaning, and nightly dishes. Mother had no respect for our very inadequate dishwasher, so we spent many nights hand washing and drying numerous pots and pans. Gratefully, it was the boys' responsibility to do dishes after our always big Sunday night meal, where relatives and guests were always welcome. We knew someone was very special in a sibling's life if they brought a date for a Sunday meal. I do remember babysitting for little Philip, born when I was ten. I was sort of a little mother to him, as Mother had back problems when Phil was very young and could not pick him up as much as he would have liked. PJ was a cute little love, and I treasured him. Unfortunately, when Doug was born, I was less kind, as Mom had suffered back surgery during her pregnancy and then experienced a frightening eclampsia at the time of Doug's birth. Doug was born premature. When he came home from the hospital, I must admit feeling a little antagonism toward this red wrinkled bundle that "almost killed my mother." Doug ended up with the greatest of personalities and was "the joy of Mom's old age." It is Doug who took over Mom's duties as family communicator after she died. The rest of us will be forever grateful to him.

All my friends idolized my gentle father. Most were patients of his and respected his kindness and genius. He was an excellent family doctor. My friends recount many home visits, when Dad came to see them when they had ear aches or sore throats. I myself felt very special when Dad took me to the office to swab a wound with merthiolate or put a stitch into my forehead after a collision with a cupboard door. Gratefully, the family was pretty healthy. Even though childhood diseases went through the family one at a time, we were very fortunate to generally avoid major illnesses or accidents. The worst memory that I had was a broken leg that Bobby experienced after chasing me home and then falling off the wall between the Coffman's house and ours. I ran into the house, after this chase, not knowing that Rob had fallen. After about thirty minutes of watching television, Grant suggested that we go outside to see why Rob had been crying for such a long time.

As a grown-up, I have heard from many that my mother was the favorite MOM of the entire neighborhood. She did have an amazing ability to focus on each person, even kids, and made them feel they were the most important person with whom she had spoken that day. She exuded warmth and sincerity. I know that as her children, each of us thought we were her favorite. Quite an accomplishment! Mother was so smart; she skipped two levels when in grade school and started college as a 16-year-old. She never finished college at Michigan State, as the Great Depression set in and the family finances became very limited. While I do not remember our parents really assisting with homework, Mother kept us on track in studies. I loved her and miss her every day of my life. I benefitted from her wisdom throughout my life. I will always miss our weekly phone calls on Saturday mornings. Tears come to my eyes as I write this; just seeing in my mind's eye the scribbled pieces of paper by the phone where Mother wrote notes as she talked with her children and friends. How lucky we were to have been her progeny!

Paula's Story

Paula passed away at age 59 of gall bladder cancer on January 3, 2007. Her story is told from consulting with her husband Robin and contributions by her siblings.

I think of Paula as being polished, unflappable, easy in her manner, a very good mother, and having many good friends. We always kidded her as a child because she refused to eat her peas. I was most distressed that she grew taller than me. One of my principles was that it was better to have loved a short man than never to have loved a-tall. But I don't remember any girls buying into that.

Grant (Author and Paula's Older Brother)
Here is a copy of Paula's own words written for our 1990 family reunion:

> To My Dear Brothers and Sisters
> I can't pick just one topic, so I offer you my random cherished memories.
> Nana's spiked heels, red lipstick and love of canasta.
> Melon balls, 37 corn fritters (and like number of water refills), roast turkey and chocolate parfaits at the West Milton Inn.
> Holy cards, glow in the dark statues of Mary, and the May procession at Corpus Christi.

Fried chicken and potato salad served at the outdoor picnic table or on the side porch.

Gigantic bonfires complete with caramel corn in the Klosterman's backyard...we'd be arrested today.

Aunt Dorothy's sweet rolls at big family celebrations.

Being the only sibling who can claim having an older brother and older sister, younger brother and younger sister.

The "big boys'" record collection, including Green Door, Autumn Leaves, and Wake Up Little Suzie.

Grandpa's rousing rendition of Happy Birthday on the piano.

Duchess and Bobby.

Driving to Indian Lake with Mom at the wheel (don't laugh – I've inherited her sense of direction).

Dad's patience with 20 patients seeking advice on his way from church to his family waiting in the wood panel station wagon.

Chrissy's distaste for dust bunnies under my bed.

The freezing sleeping porch and my appreciation of not having to slumber there.

Grandma Deger and Esther Price candy.

Being able to drive the car at night immediately after getting my driver's license. Being fifth in line does have some advantages.

And the fact that I was born on Chrissy's third birthday.

And the realization that today, being fifth in line would probably mean not being born.

Collecting tax stamps.

Dad's Fords.

Aunt Leila making noodles.

Summer afternoons swimming at Sherwood Forest.

Aunt Dorothy's garden.

The Reilings, Klostermans, Dahms, Dineens, Smiths, Jones, Wilsons, and all their wonderful offspring.

Ursuline Camp with Chris and Beth.

Our baby books.

CYO sports...the only opportunity young girls had to step on a playing field.

Charlotte Foy's Christmas tree cookie decoration. She was the Martha Stewart of her generation.

Lunch at Rikes' Department Store in downtown Dayton.

Ronnie bringing home Joyce for the first time.

The Penguin and yummy chocolate malts.

Playing bridge with the folks – and they never laughed at some of my bids.

Phil and Dougie becoming best buds.

Waking up at 5:30 AM to see the boys' choir at 6 AM Christmas morning. How easy it was to wake up and sneak a peek at the tree.... the choir was magical, the Mass endless, and Grandpa's 50-cent pieces amazingly generous.

Aunt Willa dressed up as Santa.

Mom's laugh.

Never getting yelled at for stripping and eating the cherries from the Dahms' trees.

Grant reading medical journals on dates (so we heard).

Mom's tears when we left Bobby at the seminary.

Spring Mill and corn mush.

$3 birthday money from Grandma and Grandpa.

Phil's being found under a rock (so sorry, Phil – I was awful).

E Clare hanging out with Jackie Zitt and Barb Hickey.

The 25-cent charge to borrow a blouse.

Thanksgiving morning hikes to Triangle Park or the Indian Mounds. Coming back to the wonderful aromas of the day with Grandma, Aunt Dorothy, Nana, and Mom working in the kitchen. I think of them every Thanksgiving and yearn for their companionship.

Monsignor Ansbury chastising parishioners sneaking out after Communion.

The Rec Center's ping pong tables and the Fall Festival where I won a can of peaches.

Endless outdoor games of SPUD and Hide 'n Seek.

Mother praying with us: "Jesus tender shepherd hear me, Bless your little lamb tonight. Through the darkness, please be near me, Watch my sleep till morning light. All this day your hand has led me, and I thank you for your care. You have warmed and clothed and fed me. Listen to my evening prayer." I'm sorry I didn't teach this to my children.

My friends warming to Mom's interest in their well-being – they all truly loved her.

Never getting tired of the Peach Tree story, although I wonder now how much is fact, how much is fiction.

Deger reunions.

Pardon my use of childhood names. How thankful I am to be able to look back with fondness. How lucky we are.

Love,

Paula

Chris (Paula's older sister)
The book has been written many years after our sweet sister Paula died of cancer after suffering through malignant breast cancer and then two years later, gall bladder cancer, to which

she succumbed. She was 58 when she died. Paula hurt when people complained of getting old, as she knew that she never would. Paula was wonderful. She was a generous woman who loved her family and was very close to her three children. She would have been very proud of them, as they have accomplished a great deal in their young lives. Of note, Paula quilted baby blankets and knitted sweaters for her (as yet) unborn grandchildren before she died.

In the beginning, Paula was born as the fifth child and the second girl into the Deger family. She was the only one who could claim to have an older and younger brother as well as an older and younger sister. She shared her birthday with her older, by three years, sister Chris. Sharing did not minimize her joy, as mother made the August first birthdays great occasions in our lives, making the celebrations twice as fun and exciting as might otherwise have been the case, with two cakes and often two birthday parties on that day.

Paula, whose skin was more able to tan than that of her sisters, was rather sickly and sallow when in her late toddler years. As it turns out, she had a kidney disease that affected her health. She did recover and was a very active healthy elementary school student. She even made all six CYO sports teams when in the seventh and eighth grades. Paula had many friends during her whole life. In grade school and in high school, she walked the distance to her buildings of learning with good friends, Julie Dineen and Linda Kellams. Paula loved that Linda had a birthday on April Fools Day and often made sure that Linda was reminded of her unique day. Julie, who lived across the street, and Paula spent much time together. As we all experienced, there were so many children in our Kenilworth neighborhood that all the Degers had our own friends, not really needing their siblings to be playmates. Barb

Reiling was shared by Paula and Chrissy, as she fell between the two of them in age. That worked out well, as all the Reilings were special friends for the whole family and sharing friendships was special.

In the summers, Paula, as did her sisters, spent many days at Sherwood Forest swimming pool. She was a very good swimmer and was on the swim team. She also played tennis for the Junior Tennis League of Dayton.

Being fun and adventurous opened Paula to many opportunities to take part in life in the late fifties and early sixties. She loved concerts and attended sports activities at Chaminade and sock hops at the school. She also went to CYODA on Friday nights. Paula attended Julienne High School for three years. As a senior she transferred to Ursuline Academy in Brown County, Ohio. That was a magical place where all three girls attended summer camp and later became camp counselors. It is unsure why Paula got the special opportunity to attend the boarding school, but her sisters were a little green with envy.

Ron (Paula's older brother, upon his last visit to see Paula before her death)
What do you say to a loved one when you are seeing them for the last time? This question was constantly on my mind during the week before starting the trip to see sister Paula in Spokane.

My thoughts kept going back to my last trip to see her in October, 2004. At that time, she had been diagnosed with a second cancer and had undergone a series of chemotherapies. At dinner on Saturday night, she announced that three months ago, her doctor had given her three months to live. But here she was alive and looking pretty good even if her hair was shorter and she was a little thinner.

On Wednesday afternoon (10/08/06) at about 1:30 PM, I began my trek from Dayton to the Cincinnati airport. The drive would take over an hour and I wanted to arrive two hours before my 4:47 PM flight. A long solitary drive is a good time to think of what I'd say to Paula the next day. Still no magic words of wisdom came to me.

The flight from Cincinnati to Salt Lake City and then on to Spokane took over six hours. I got to my hotel about 9 PM Spokane time. I had been in transit about 11 hours and still had no inspiration on what to say.

The next morning, Robin picked me up at the hotel and we drove to their home. Robin updated me on her condition as we took the scenic drive through the city, by Manitou Park, past Robin's country club and up the valley to their home. What a pillar of strength Robin epitomizes. I could not imagine the trauma he has gone through these last four years of Paula's fight with cancer.

When we walked in the front door, Paula's voice from her upstairs bedroom welcomed us. I had to wait a few minutes for Robin to go up and help her come down to her living room chair beside the big picture window. After she settled into her chair, I was finally able to give her a big hug and a kiss.

Poor thing, she looked nowhere near the sister I had seen two years ago. She was much thinner, looked frail, and was in a lot of discomfort. Right away after sitting down she became nauseous and had to vomit up some gastric fluids. She had a procedure done on Monday to drain these fluids into a bag, but apparently it wasn't working then. Happily, when Robin investigated, he found the line to her bag had been twisted and this led to the drain not working.

Paula had become the bag lady. The pouch in front of her contained three bags, all of which needed attention during the day. Robin drained them several times during the day. In addition, he replaced her IV feeding bag and gave her a variety of medications during the day. Robin had been scheduled for a long workday, but the surgery was cancelled due to a health problem developed by his patient. Luckily, he was home most of the day to attend Paula and visit with me.

Through the morning, I sat on a couch next to Paula. Discussions covered a wide variety of points. I had brought some genealogy records showing our ancestors in the four surnames of Deger, Hochwalt, Grant, and Briggs. My intention was to make sure her kids had a record of our family tree. At some point, I also mentioned that she could take the listings with her and look up some of our ancestors on the "other side."

I had also brought some pictures of my grandkids. Two had Morgan in the sweater that Paula had so graciously knitted for her. Two had Blake in the blanket she had made for him. One picture was of Paula and some of us at Manitou Park in 2004. She was standing on a bench with her arms outstretched, with us in the background. I call it my "Titanic Paula" picture because it reminds me of the scene from the movie *Titanic*, where Kate Winslett is standing on the bow of the *Titanic* with her arms outstretched.

I also showed her some pictures of a recent family gathering at Dan and Connie O'Brien's southern Indiana farm. While there, we gathered together to form a big Paula hug, and I wanted Paula to know of it.

I was a little apprehensive about showing grandkid pictures to her. I knew that she wanted to see her own grandkids. During the day she mentioned that she was disappointed she would neither see her kids get married nor see any of her grandchildren. She said she thought she would be a good grandmother. I know she would have been a great one.

We also looked at an old NCR Company newsletter detailing the gift of the Carillon by Col. And Mrs. Deeds. It contained articles about the Carillon and its construction. Our old neighbor, Robert Kline, was pictured. One of my grade-school classmate's (Carol Kneer) mother and father, both NCR employees, had been married and were pictured in the newsletter. Joe Klosterman, the grandfather of the Kenilworth Klostermans, was also pictured. I recognized other names and hoped Paula would likewise find names of people she recognized.

Another book I had brought was a new one written by a local historian that showed hundreds of pictures of Dayton. The pictures brought back a lot of memories. We did not dwell too long on any of these books, newsletters, pictures, or records. Paula grew tired of reading. From time to time she would doze off for a few minutes.

She also got a plethora of phone calls. Both Haley and Cassy were on trips. Haley was headed to Florida for an "Iron Man" competition and checked in from several airports and when she arrived in Florida. Cassy was headed to Boston to visit a college friend. She was likewise checking in with Mom to report her progress and to check on Paula. I was sorry to have missed them.

Around noon Robin and I sat down for lunch. While we were eating, Paula's priest stopped by to discuss funeral arrangements. This is not the easiest thing for one to talk about, but Paula was as strong as ever. The priest left a few books on Catholic funerals. Paula and I discussed some favorite songs. I did tell her that I did not think I would say anything at her funeral because it would probably get too emotional. I normally do not have a problem speaking in public. However, I did not do well at Dad's memorial service at Marie Joseph and would not want to repeat my performance at Paula's funeral.

We continued our off-again, on-again discussions during the afternoon. We saw a coyote walking up their driveway. We also saw a number of quail feeding in their yard.

Robin had to go to the office for a few hours. A neighbor (Juliane Sullivan) dropped by in the late afternoon to check up on Paula. She is a nurse and asked a lot of detailed questions on how Paula was doing. She made a number of notes about Paula's status. Juliane is a very caring individual, and the strength of friendship between her and Paula was remarkable. A little later, another friend, Charlotte Oliva, dropped by with her two daughters and they brought dinner for Robin and me. Once again, the depth of friendship was very visible among Paula, Charlotte, and her daughters. Past family ski trips were remembered with laughter and fondness.

After dinner, we watched a little TV and talked a little more. Robin had to attend to more medications and get Paula reconnected to her IV feeding apparatus. Around 9:00 PM we decided that it was time for me to leave, as Paula would be going to bed in about a half hour. This gave Robin time to get me to the motel and return home.

Saying goodbye was hard. We hugged, kissed, told each other we loved one another, and then Robin and I left. A lot of the ride back was in silence. I was reflecting on the day and was also afraid of getting too emotional in expressing what a great job I thought Robin was doing. We did discuss Paula's condition and prognosis. Apparently, her kidneys and liver were strong. However, the blockages and the drains were preventing her from absorbing nutrition from her IV feedings. She could not last long under these conditions. Paula had not given up yet.

The next morning, Robin ran me to the airport. Hugging another man is not something I grew up doing. However, I did not hesitate hugging Robin as we parted at the airport.

The trip home also took a long time and gave me a lot to think about. Did I say the right things? Did I do something I should not have done? What more should I have said? I don't know. I do know that anyone that has so many people caring for her in her final illness has to be a pretty good friend, neighbor, sister, mother, and person. I take great comfort in knowing she is being well cared for.

Her physical appearance is not the beauty of years past. I will tell you one thing. The image that I have of her as I write this note is of her sitting drawn and weak in her chair and then looking up and smiling as I was leaving. The smile was a thing of beauty.

Beth's Story

I was seven years old when our family moved to the big red brick house at 724 Kenilworth Avenue. It was the early Christmases that we enjoyed in that house that I frequently think back on. It was still a time when we awoke early to drive in the cold and dark to Corpus Christi Church by 5 AM to hear the boys' choir sing carols before the 6 AM Mass. I was especially proud that it was our Grandpa Deger playing the organ and directing the choir at those services. I don't remember much else about the Mass since I was probably more focused on getting home and opening our Christmas gifts.

Normally we arrived home from church at daybreak around 7 AM. One Christmas as we pulled up to our driveway, Santa Claus was standing on our snowy front lawn ringing bells and welcoming us home. It turned out it was our Great Aunt Willa visiting from Arizona and not Santa, but you couldn't have convinced me that I didn't see Santa in person that day. Nana's sister Willa looked and sounded more like Santa than any of the pretenders we had our pictures taken with at the Santa-Land in Rike's Department store in downtown Dayton.

When we got home from Mass and before we could take off our coats, Paula and I would be discussing who would get to wake up Phil and Doug to let them know Santa had left us our gifts. Remembering the faces of our little brothers as they descended the stairs and ran into the living room to see all the gifts under the tree always makes me smile.

Something I remember about Christmas trees was how hard it was to wait until a day or two before Christmas for Dad to take us to the Siebenthaler Nursery on Philadelphia Drive to select our favorite fir. Having the patience to wait until December 23 was not easy when most of our friends obtained their trees weeks before Christmas.

As we sibs know, our Mother and Father were extremely generous with gifts. Even with the eight of us, it was easy to find our individual gifts under the tree by how they were arranged. It was as if the space under the tree was divided into individual slices like a huge pizza. Each of us had our own pile of presents starting with Grant's on one side and wrapping around the tree ending up with Doug's on the other. I always knew I could find my pile of goodies arranged lovingly between Phil's and Paula's.

Our delicious turkey dinners followed later in the day with normally 20 plus folks around the dining room table. It was always fun to meet the special dates my older sibs would invite to join us. I would often observe the various couples holding hands under the table and be terribly amused.

By the time I was a teenager, we thankfully changed our tradition of getting up at 4 AM for Christmas Mass. Eventually, whoever was home late on Christmas Eve drove out to St. Leonard's Seminary in Centerville for Midnight Mass. How lovely and special it was to begin Mass observing the Friars file in two at a time into church dressed in their brown robes with big hoods singing in Gregorian chant. I'm not sure why we chose to attend Mass at St. Leonard's, but I'm glad we did.

Whether beginning our Christmas celebrations at Mass at 6 AM or midnight, those Christmases in Dayton with family will always evoke many warm and amazing memories.

Phil's Story

I was born on November 4, 1955, the seventh child in my family. I attended Corpus Christi Catholic School through the eighth grade, and then Chaminade-Julienne High School where I graduated in 1974. I continued my Catholic education at Thomas More College, and after dropping out and then later returning, I received a BA in Business Administration in 1981.

During my college age years, I lived in the Denver, Colorado, area for a summer, where two of my sisters were living at the time. I worked at a Coca Cola plant that summer. As a boy I worked at delivering newspapers, and later at Rike's Department store, AAA license bureau, Siebenthaler's Nursery, *Dayton Daily News* delivery truck driver, and telemarketer for a marketing research firm. In 1981 I went to work for the U.S. Postal Service and retired from there in November of 2012.

I was MVP for my Little League baseball one year. I was in Cub Scouts, Boy Scouts, and Explorers. I lettered in tennis in high school one year. I made the Dean's List in my junior year of college. I ran three half-marathons and participated in various 5 K and 10 K races as a runner. I won third place in the Turkey Trot one year and second place one year later in my weight division. I won first place in the Chaminade-Julienne 5 K race in my age division. I got the Safe Driving Award at the Post Office, and I was given a "Mailman Extraordinaire" award from the Wales Drive Neighborhood Association in 2005 by a wonderful group of my patrons.

I think my greatest accomplishment was turning my life around in 1984, after my divorce, and kicking an alcohol and drug problem. I met my wonderful wife, Terri, in late 1989, and we were married in May 1992. We have been happily married for 25 years and I am blessed and thankful every day that God brought Terri into my life. We blended our families and five beautiful young ladies – Lori, Kristi, Julie, Molly, and Beth – into one big happy family. Tragically, we lost our beautiful daughter Kristi Marie in May 2014 to cancer. She will always be in our hearts and we feel certain she is watching over our now-growing family from Heaven. We have been blessed with seven terrific grandchildren – Addison, Noah, Chase, Faith, Owen, Ethan, and Jake. They are our pride and joy and we love spending time with them. The other precious addition to our family is our little dog, Laney. She is a sweetheart and we love her so very much.

In addition to family time, I enjoy swimming and walking, which has taken the place of my running, and occasionally biking and hiking – but not to the extent that I did in the past when I climbed twin 14,000-foot peaks in Colorado or biked from our house in the northern part of Dayton where we lived down along the Miami River to the southern suburb of West Carrollton. I also spend much of my time gardening and taking care of my fairly large yard. I really enjoy reading, especially historical non-fiction and presidential biographies. My favorite author is David McCullough. I visit the library regularly to read the business newspapers and magazines, and I enjoy watching and reading about the stock market since I have been an avid follower and small-time investor since 1993. I was an usher at St. Rita Catholic Church, Mom and Dad's parish for many years, before we moved to Kettering in 2004. I have been a life-long fan of the Cincinnati Reds, the Cleveland Browns, and more recently the Dayton Dragons, our hometown minor league baseball team.

Some of my fondest memories growing up in the Deger household are family Christmases, backyard Easter egg hunts, family vacations, trips to Indian Lake, going to Reds games and U.D. basketball games with Dad, getting into Dad's Cokes and Hershey bars from his office, visits to the deli on Salem Avenue on Sunday nights, Dad driving us to school when we were young and how I hid behind the chair when it was time to go to school, Mom's ice cream treats, Mom's letter writing, Mom's care packages sent to me in college, Mom's chocolate chip cookies and other favorites she made for us. I also remember getting help from Dad for our paper route deliveries on Sunday mornings, then going to early Mass at Corpus Christi, followed by breakfast with Dad at Frisch's. I remember Little League, soccer, Boy Scouts, and playing baseball and basketball with my friends and neighbors for hours at a time. I remember my running days as a young adult and how good it made me feel. I would still be running today if my knees didn't dictate that I walk now instead.

I have happy memories of bringing Molly and Beth to their grandparents every other Sunday when I had the girls with me. Mom especially made those visits very special. I remember my Mom's caring ways, her infectious laugh, and the way she cared for and loved everyone. She was a good sport when I attempted to say things to make her blush. One special memory I have of Mom is that on my first day of delivering mail, my trainer let me deliver the mail to my own parents' home on Knollview. I'll never forget the big smile on Mom's face and the pride in her eyes as she waited on the front porch holding her letters that she wanted to give to the mailman, and the joy in my heart as I walked up to her and delivered her mail. Another memory of Mom that is special to me is that the very last afghan that Mom made (and she made one for just about everyone) was for Terri, my bride-to-be, and she gave it to her at Christmas, just a little over a month before she died.

I have some good memories of spending time with Dad in the years he lived at Maria Joseph Retirement Center / Nursing Home. Whether it was taking him out to dinner at MCL Cafeteria once a week or just sitting with him in his apartment listening to a ballgame, and many times dozing off in the chair with him doing the same, I am grateful to have spent those years with him and getting to know him better before he died.

I am forever grateful that I was given such a wonderful family to grow up in, such a happy childhood, blessing in my adult years, and I continue to love and cherish all my brothers and sisters to this day!

Doug's Story

I was born on April 30, 1957. I was two months premature, and Mom was seriously ill during my birth. Thank God she survived and provided me 34 excellent years of love and guidance. I was blessed to have two amazing parents and seven older brothers and sister, all of whom I value and am very proud of and enjoy conversing with on a semi-regular basis.

My first job, at ten, was a paper route that included very early morning as well as afternoon routes. I did that for four years, and worked retail and at AAA through my teens. Although resistant in the beginning, I was enrolled in a theatrical group of kids in grade school and surprisingly enjoyed participating in over 13 plays up through eighth grade. I thank Mom to this day for encouraging me to do that, as the enjoyment and excitement and the subsequent people skills I learned from those experiences have benefited me throughout my sales career and shaped my positive personality to this day.

I was the last of eight siblings to attend Corpus Christi School as well as the last male sibling to attend Chaminade-Julienne High School. I was a four-year varsity tennis player as well as MVP my senior season. I also enjoyed teaching tennis during the summer months and through most of my college career. I enjoyed participating in tennis tournaments as well as the comradery of playing with a group of tennis savvy and now lifelong friends.

I started my college adventure at Miami University after high school and ended up graduating from Wright State University with a BS in Marketing. I had some success and enjoyment selling computers and related equipment my first jobs out of college, through my 20s, 30s, and 40s. For several years I worked as an inside sales representative nationwide for a worldwide crane company called Konecranes. Now I sell check scanners to banks for Panini Company.

I have many fond memories of my siblings, one of the best being Christmas time in grade school. It didn't get any better than the house smelling of ginger bread, and the excitement and mystery surrounding the impending visit of St. Nick. The home at 724 Kenilworth was always alive with music, large family and friend get-togethers, late night TV watching and overall, just a consistent, positive place to be. And like Mom and Dad mentioned many times, Christmas was always some of the best times of the year. God bless "Bob and Winnie."

In our neighborhood, growing up, we were told that being a part of a family of ten, with seven older siblings, that this was not such a big deal. In the streets surrounding our Kenilworth home, and along with our 28 straight years of Deger attendance at Corpus Christi grade school, we were sometimes dwarfed by families of ten, twelve, and a few families of fourteen and one with fifteen family members.

What a great opportunity to learn from and interact with all types of families and family backgrounds. Two of my best friends in life only lived five doors from me. Life-long bonds were formed in and around the neighborhood that I called home for over eighteen years.

We would ride bikes, play all kinds of sports, play board games, go the Triangle Park for an entire day at a time, and play tennis, soccer, football, baseball, and interact with nature, spend hours examining bugs and snakes, chasing butterflies and lightning bugs. In the summertime, we would wake up, put on our Converse tennis shoes, leave the house at nine, get on our bike, tear up the neighborhood and surrounding areas and make sure we were always home for dinner at six. Parenting may have been a little different in those days.

My memories of my siblings come in to focus as early as five. The three oldest boys--Grant, Ron, and "Bobbi"--were already forging their paths in life and weren't around a lot. They were all focused on coming adulthood, attending college, and planning life. I remember being so proud of my oldest brother, Grant. He was already in college the year I was born. After getting his undergrad degree at UD, one fond memory I have is the family going to his medical fraternity house in Cincinnati for a spaghetti dinner fund raiser. The whole family was so proud, and what a solid group of young men. Grant would go on to become a doctor, a very positive role model.

Ron had joined the Marines after his UD degree and went on to get his master's in business. I remember his wedding to Joyce Niecamp, an amazing lady to whom he has been married 54 years. Ron wore his Marine dress whites, along with his side armor.

Brother Rob was heading towards a deployment in Vietnam. And when he came back, he pursued and attained both his masters and PHD advanced degrees. I recall when he was in high school at Chaminade, Rob would gather together with his friends in the living rooms at 724 Kenilworth. He would play guitar, sing along with everyone in attendance, and tell jokes. Talk about being the life a party, he was all that.

I also remember visiting him at Indiana University, where Rob was pursuing his PHD, and at the time he was newly engaged. I recall going with Mom and Dad and meeting his finance and her younger sister. I was in my early to mid-teens and was overwhelmed by such a major college campus. Wow, that was very exciting to be exposed to that environment and what it represented. At that moment, I wanted to bypass high school and go right to college. Least of all was the fact that I developed a major crush on Rob's finance's younger sister. I never wanted that visit to end.

When Rob was attending grad school in New Mexico, he was also an amateur pilot. I will never forget the day Rob took our Mother, Phil, and me up in small plane several thousands of feet up in the air. I can still see my Mother's face when the door of the plane right next to her popped open. Phil and I were so young, we didn't seem understand the seriousness of that moment. We never felt threatened or in danger. Needless to say, Mom was very animated and excited about the door opening. Rob just calmly reached across and pulled the door shut and we continued our flight.

Sisters Chris, Paula, and Beth were around the Kenilworth homestead the most. I have so many wonderful memories of spending time and being with and cared for by my sisters. Some of my favorite Christmas memories were where Chris would make gingerbread houses and related Christmas decorations. She was always very creative. The smell of ginger bread would fill the house and she would sometimes let me eat some of the excess bread.

Sisters Paula and Beth would wake Phil and me up on Christmas morning. We would race down the front steps to the living room, where the night before the decorations and Christmas tree were fully set up and covered with lights and decorations. What a beautiful sight to a Santa-believing and holiday-loving youngster. The same area around the tree that was barren the night before, on Christmas morning would be filled with presents. Santa (Mom and Dad) was always too generous, but it was always a very happy time of year.

Being the youngest, my pile of gifts was to the far left, with Phil's gifts next to mine, then Beth etc., all around the tree for the Deger eight. Most Christmases Dad would buy fresh trees and build some aesthetically pleasing and hypnotic fires in the fireplace that was right in the center of the living room. We would all spend hours looking at the fires, being together, talking, and enjoying the holiday warmth.

The girls were saddled with watching out for their younger siblings. They provided Phil and me time and joy. They gave up some of their "time" to support and help their younger siblings. Phil and I greatly appreciated that in later life and realized what giving and caring sisters we had. And needless to say, we all miss our beloved sister Paula, who went to be with the Lord in 2007.

Brother Phil always was and continues to be my best friend in the world. We shared all of our growing up experiences together that started when I was very young, when Phil and I would fight like brothers often do. In early grade school, he was always much taller and weighed more than I did. So, when fighting, all he had to do was sit on top of me and I was unable to do anything to fight back. As we got closer to high school, I started lifting weights and the playing field was more level in later life.

When I was seven or eight, among other summer games and projects, one summer we decided to make bows and arrows from the bushes and related foliage around our home. We would take some bush branches and whittle them into a bow with twine and also create some arrows. Phil accidentally shot an arrow into my lower leg. At that moment I was kind shocked to see an arrow sticking out of my leg, but it didn't bother me until Mom came out of the kitchen to see what was going on.

As soon as I saw my mother, the tears began to flow. As I knew, love and attention would flow from that amazing lady and everything would be alright. Mom was the most people-oriented, loving and sincerely interested in everyone, woman you would ever meet. She would call me the "joy of her old age" and always introduce me as her "baby." At first, I would bemoan her introducing me as her baby, but in later life, I came to enjoy, appreciate, and live for those introductions.

Dad was already in his 60s when I found the love of tennis, as he had, and was able to share hours on the courts and time with my father. When I was in the second grade and broke my wrist playing in the side yard, it was around supper time, early summer. Mom had just made supper and Dad had me lay down on the living room couch as he finished his dinner.

After dinner, he took me to Good Samaritan hospital, fixed my wrist, put it in a cast, and when I awoke from the surgery, I remember saying "Thanks Dad!" Good Sam is closing this month after 86 years of service in Dayton, and I know all my sibs either studied or worked there at some time in their youth, very sad to see it close.

As the last of Deger eight, I have always been very proud and fascinated by the interactions, goals, personalities, interests, intelligence, and directions of all those whom I call my older siblings. What an amazing collection of good, positive human beings, I have always been proud to be a member of this gang of "eight." In this day and age of smaller families, you don't realize how lucky it was to be born into, and become a member of, such a wonderful group.

I treasure and value being a sibling in the Deger environment and look forward to many more years being with and talking to my family members well into my retirement years. God bless all the Degers and related families, and here's to more amazing life experiences in the coming decades.

Outcomes

On precisely April 26, 2018, Chaminade/Julienne High School awarded the Deger Family its legacy award. Our grandmother Agnes Hochwalt Deger had entered Julienne's precursor, Notre Dame Academy, in 1902. Our father, Robert, finished Chaminade High School in 1930. We eight siblings (Great Eight) attended Chaminade or Julienne for 22 straight years. Then my brother Phil's three step-daughters graduated from the now-combined Chaminade/ Julienne. The last daughter, Julie, finished in 1999. In all, there was a 97-year span of Degers attending Dayton's Catholic High School.

All of the "Great Eight" graduated from college, and five of us have advanced degrees. I have an MD, Ron an MBA, Rob a PhD in history, Chris a master's degree in Nursing, Paula a degree in Journalism, Beth a master's degree in Library Science and 50+ credit hours in Horticulture, and Phil and Doug degrees in Business.

Epilogue

I hope you enjoyed sharing in this post-WW II history of Dayton as seen by eight siblings growing up in a middle-class Catholic neighborhood. It was a kinder time, marked by strong family ties and more open religious expression.

Writing this book has intensified my affection for my family, friends, and country. I give thanks to God for the beneficence of really good parents, siblings, and schools. Providence gave "The Great Eight" education, opportunity, and freedom to live the American Dream. I have pleasant memories to take with me all my days.

I cannot thank my brothers and sisters enough. Ronald Thomas gave copiously of his time and efforts, especially in the areas of genealogy and old photographs. Robert John Jr., Christine Louise, Elizabeth Claire, Philip Joseph, and Douglas William generously wrote their stories and were patient when I interrupted with questions. We loved and remember our sister Paula Ann who died over 11 years ago and whose memories were reconstructed by us. Many hugs go to my wife Candice for her forbearance as I whiled away time trying to construct a book, a new project for me.

APPENDIX OF CURRICULUM VITAE / RESUMES

Dear reader. This may or may not be a boring portion of the book, but herein are the details of our professional lives and personal pursuits as adults.

Grant (author)

Grant

Personal

- Birthday: September 15, 1939, Dayton, Ohio
- Family: wife Candice, children 6 (three stepsons)

Personal Interests

- Choir singing: Assumption Church Bellingham, WA and St. Bernard Parish Scottsdale, AZ
- Chorale singing: Whatcom Chorale, Bellingham, WA, North Valley Chorale Scottsdale, AZ
- Sang with the North Valley Chorale at Carnegie Hall, New York City, November 2017
- Contract Bridge: Life Master December 2015, Bronze Life Master, January 2017
- Bicycling, gym exercises, gardening, and years ago racket-ball and mountain climbing
- Voracious reader: love English literature the most

Education

- Bachelor of Science, University of Dayton, 1961
- Medical degree, University of Cincinnati, 1965

Rotating Internship

- Good Samaritan Hospital, Dayton, Ohio, 1965 – 1966

Internal Medicine Residency

- Mayo Clinic, Rochester, Minnesota, 1966 – 1969

Military

- Captain U.S. Air Force, Fairchild Regional Hospital, Spokane, WA, 1969 – 1971

- Vice Chairman (as a civilian), Medical Staff, Oak Harbor Navy Hospital, 1997 – 1998

Practice

- Private practice, Internal Medicine and Nephrology, July 1971 to September 1996, Bellingham, WA
- Oak Harbor Navy Hospital, Whidbey Island, WA, 1996 – 1998
- Consultant to Social Security Disability Hearings, 1997 – 2006
- Whatcom Occupational Health 1999 – 2002
- Whatcom County Jail Physician, 2000 – 2006
- Medical Director, Washington State Department of Corrections 2006 – 2007, Olympia, WA
- Retired October 2007, age 68

Board Certification

- Internal Medicine, 1972
- Nephrology, 1974
- Medical Review Officer (illicit drug testing), 1999
- Certified Correctional Health Professional (CCHP), 2004

Fellow

- Studies in Tropical Medicine – scholarship from the World Health Organization, Summer, 1963
- American College of Physicians, (FACP) 1976 -2008

Honors / Awards

- Alpha Omega Alpha Honor Society (graduated top 10% in medical school), 1964
- North Pacific Society of Internal Medicine - invited 1974 to this honorary society which included leading internists from Washington, Idaho, Oregon, and British Columbia
- National Commission on Correctional Health Care (NCCHC) "Jail Facility of the Year" award, October 2005
- Community Service Award, American College of Physicians, Washington Chapter, 2006

- Legacy Family Award, Chaminade Catholic High School, Dayton, Ohio, April 2018

Director

- St. Lukes Hospital Hypertension Clinic, 1975 – 1991
- Supervised monthly physician lecture series, Consultants in Medicine Clinic, 1992 – 1996
- Bellingham Police and Fire Department Pension Board Physician 1972 – 1996
- Emergency Medical and Health Branch Director for Whatcom County, WA, 2003 – 2006
- Washington Department of Corrections (Medical), 2006 -2007

Committee

- Sub-Committee on Rural Hypertension, National Institute of Health, 1979
- Washington State Governor's Council, American College of Physicians 1994 – 1998

President

- Washington State Society of Internal Medicine, 1980
- Whatcom County Medical Society, 1981
- Catholic Community Services, 1989
- Bellingham City Council, 2005

Community Service

- Catholic Community Services Board, 1985 – 1989
- Rotary International, 1989 – 1991
- Tree Planting Project, Sunrise Neighborhood, 1996
- Chairman Assumption Church and School Renovation, a $2 million project, 1998 – 2000
- Whatcom Symphony Board, 2000 – 2002
- Bellingham City Council, 4th Ward, January 2002 – December 2005
- Economic Development Council Board, 2002 – 2003
- The Opportunity Council Board, 2002 – 2003
- Bellingham Parks Board, 2002 – 2004
- Mt. Baker Kidney Center board, 2004 – 2006
- Whatcom Chorale board, 2010 – 2014

Publications

- Pneumoperitoneum. *Ohio State Medical Journal* 63:67, 1966.
- Peritoneal Dialysis in Acute Uric Acid Nephropathy. *Mayo Clinic Proceedings* 47:189 – 192, 1972
- Aflatoxin – Human Colon Carcinogenesis. *Annals of Internal Medicine* 85;204, 1976
- Hypertension Control in a Medium-Sized Community. Thesis prepared for the American College of Physicians, 1976
- Control of Hypertension in a Medium-Sized Community. *Western Journal of Medicine* 130:184 – 187, 1979
- Terazosin: An Effective Once-Daily Monotherapy for the treatment of Hypertension. *American Journal of Medicine* 80:68-72, 1986
- Comparison of the Safety and Efficacy of Once-Daily Terazosin versus Twice-Daily Prazosin for the Treatment of Mild to Moderate hypertension. *American Journal of Medicine* 80:68-72, 1986
- Long-Term Experience with Terazosin for Treatment of Mild to Moderate Hypertension, *American Journal of Medicine* 80:82-87, 1986
- Effect of Terazosin on Serum Lipids. *American Journal of Medicine* 80: 82-87, 1986
- The Safety and Efficacy of Once-Daily Nifedipine Coat-Core in Combination with Atenolol in Hypertensive Patients. *Clinical Therapeutics* 15:976-987, 1993
- The Antihypertensive and Lipid Lowering Treatment to Prevent Heart Attack Trial (ALLHAT): Clinical Center Recruitment Experience, *Journal of the Society for Clinical Trials* 22:659-669, December 2001
- The Enduring Menace of MRSA: Incidence, Treatment, and Prevention in a County Jail, *Journal of Correctional Health Care*, Vol.15, No. 3 174-178, July 2009

Clinical Research:

- Stage III clinical trial of acebutolol (Sectral); 10 hypertensive patients. Ives Company, protocol #MDS 304, 1979
- Stage III clinical trial of terazosin (Hytrin); 25 hypertensive patients, Abbott Company protocol #MDS 304, 1979
- Stage III clinical trial of terazosin (Hytrin); 7 hypertensive patients. Abbott Company, protocol # M81-005, 1982
- Stage III clinical trial of terazosin (Hytrin); 30 hypertensive patients, Abbott Company, protocol #M83-012, 1983
- Stage II clinical trial of terazosin (Hytrin); 10 hypertensive patients. Abbott Company, protocol # M83-013, 1983
- Stage III clinical trial of captopril (Capoten); 13 hypertensive patients. Squibb Company, protocol #23982-011, 1985
- Stage III clinical trial of zofenopril; 17 hypertensive patients. Squibb Company, protocol #21, 974-16, 1987
- Stage III clinical trial of nifedipine (Adalat CC); 16 hypertensive patients. Miles Company, protocol #D89-018, 1989
- Stage III clinical trial of amlodipine (Norvasc); Cardiovascular Community Trial. 13 hypertensive patients. Pfizer Company, protocol #D90-S-6472, 1992
- Stage III clinical trial of Fluvastatin (Lescol); 8 hyperlipidemic patients. Sandoz company, protocol #XUC-374, 1993
- Stage III clinical trial of doxazosin (Cardura); Mild-Moderate Hypertension with Symptoms of Benign Prostatic Hypertrophy. 30 patients. Pfizer Company, protocol #R-0388, 1994
- ALLHAT. Antihypertensive and Lipid Lowering treatment to prevent Heart Attack Trial; 114 patients. National Institute of Health, 1994-2002

Ron

Background

My successful general management background includes direction of plants, companies, divisions, and groups of companies international operations, management of manufacturing operations, designing products, planning growth, implementing computer systems, service on Boards of Directors, and handling finances and legal issues. I oversaw operations, directed the development of new product lines, handled sales functions and was a major player in marketing and market planning. I also established plans that expanded companies. I created inventory control, sales reporting, and standard cost systems. As well, I worked with banks and performed extensive financial analysis.

With my breadth of experience, I am able to see problems clearly and develop innovative solutions. I prioritize well, set goals wisely and plan activities in advance. I am competitive and challenge my people to succeed. I am also fair, open, and honest with my employees and counsel them so that they do a better job. I effectively delegate responsibility to my subordinates, and I do not tolerate wasteful operations. In addition, I deal well with people and possess the ability to take the edge off of tough situations.

Work Experience

- Interpreter of Dayton History at Carillon Park, Dayton, Ohio, 1998-2016

Responsible for interpreting individual exhibits and conducting tours of all of the exhibits in this twenty-three building, sixty-five acre privately funded Historical Park. Visitors to the Park include school groups, family groups, business and military groups, and the general public. I have been considered by Park management to be one of the better guides in terms of knowledge of the exhibits and presentation skills. I developed a new way to demonstrate to schoolchildren how the Wright Brothers controlled their planes and then conduct simulated flights from Carillon Park to various locations.

- Ad Products of Dayton – Part Time Bookkeeper and Sales Representative, 2003-2016

    Responsible for preparation of the general ledger of the Corporation. I am also responsible for Accounts Payable and Accounts Receivable. I prepare all checks for the company and collect and deposit the Receivables. I decide how to invest corporate funds and the allocation among Checking, Savings, and Certificates of Deposit. As a Sales Representative, I act as a commissioned salesman in selling promotional products to businesses, medical personnel, government agencies, churches and schools.

- Shred-It, Owner and General Manager, Springboro, Ohio, 1995-1996

    Responsible for the start up and successful operation of a new branch of North America's largest mobile paper shredding company. This branch operated in a franchised area covering Southwest Ohio and Northern Kentucky. As General Manager I grew the customer base from zero to over 300 accounts. Revenues increased from zero to the annualized rate of $400,000 with pretax profit of 11.2% for the last accounting period. This branch was third best out of forty-one in revenue generation per truck and twelfth in terms of revenue per driver hour. Negotiated an SBA loan and met all credit obligations on a timely basis.

- Waste Management – State President of Oklahoma - Tulsa, Oklahoma, 1994-1995

  Responsible to Corporate operations in the State of Oklahoma, consisting of three landfills, two waste hauling divisions, and two recycling centers. I found that the Tulsa hauling division was the biggest problem area, made organizational changes, and developed a cost containment and productivity program for the division. Reviewed financial statements and conducted monthly operational reviews of each organization.

  Successfully won a bid for the start up of the Oklahoma City contract, one of the largest ever won by the parent corporation, with trash pickup for 80,000 homes and recycling pick up for 137,000 homes. In Oklahoma City, we set up a new distribution center for the hauling division, tripled the division's truck fleet, and set up a new recycling center for the hauling division, tripled the division's truck fleet, and set up a new recycling center. Grew pretax profit from 37% of budget to 120.6% of budget including a $100,000+ write off. Grew state revenue 66% in one year and attained budgeted price increase goals. The Tulsa Division had a 35% greater YTD Revenue than previously, with earnings up $171,000. Achieved excellent environmental audits for the landfills and obtained numerous contracts.

- Waste Management of Illinois – West, Vice President of Sales and Marketing, 1992-1994

  Managed the heads of three previous sales divisions and molded them into a cohesive team. Aggressively sought out increases in market share, developed the sales force, and oversaw municipal sales. Consolidated two divisions and 60% of the third division and moved the sales department into a single location in Batavia, Illinois. Reorganized the department into nine sales territories, and a municipal marketing function, negotiated specific goals and started target account programs with each representative. Set up a sales reporting system and handled a major acquisition.

Implemented two successful price increases that grew revenue $4,800,000 per year, and a third increase that brought in $3,000,000 per year greatly increasing division profitability. Acted as key account representative for the Ameritech account in the Chicago metropolitan area with over 240 locations and $300,000 in revenue. Developed a new marketing method for selling roll off service to homebuilders and a system for tracking financial data. In addition, negotiated a recycling/waste removal program for a national account.

- Waste Management – Senior Director, Advanced Technology Department, 1990-1992

    Managed a new waste management collection system (WMS System) project with an ultimate budget of $40,000,000 to replace traditional hauling equipment. In addition, handled a number of other projects such as a cart dumping mechanism attached to front and rear loading trucks and a quick unloading roll off trailer. Organized the department, managed new product design and the start up and sales operation of the new equipment. Set up a system to track product sales and a pricing formula for carts and containers. Worked with international and domestic manufacturers to make the products more reliable.

    Enabled the cart manufacturer to become the second largest in the United States. Used the WMS System as a marketing tool, giving the corporation a competitive advantage. The rear loader dumping mechanism yielded over 20% more productivity and became mandatory in the corporation. Successfully introduced a grid pad system, scales for trucks that weighed the trash as it was being lifted and dumped into the truck, and automatic tarpers for roll off units that also became the corporate standard. In addition, directed the design of a computerized routing system.

- Waste Management – Regional Vice President of Operations/Assistant to the Region Manager – 1989-1990

    Built up the Minnesota, Wisconsin, and Canadian operations and prepared and bid for a $1,000,000,000 project. Conducted monthly operating reviews with Wisconsin, Minnesota, and Canadian Managers, and developed a management training and succession plan. Subsequently managed eight Wisconsin hauling divisions. Focused on management and marketing problems in the Milwaukee market, and restructured the divisions. In addition, I sought out acquisition candidates.

    Solidified the sales efforts of the two large Milwaukee Divisions. Returned the Milwaukee hauling companies to profitability, assured they were operating ahead of budget in pretax profit, and improved productivity. Discontinued several money losing ventures. Successfully relocated the Green Bay division into a new facility. Initiated acquisition negotiations with a large Madison hauling company and doubled the size of the Madison Division through this purchase.

- Danis Industries Corporation – Vice President – Dayton, Ohio – 1988-1989

    Invited to rejoin company to investigate acquisition opportunities to continue the company's growth and allow it to diversify into another business segment. Worked with approximately $20,000,000 in corporate cash for this $400,000,000 privately held company. Set up a network of Merger and Acquisition brokers, accountant, and lawyers to provide acquisition leads. Evaluated over 100 opportunities for the company and presented six acquisition candidates. When the corporation decided to sell off some of its business instead of acquiring new ones, worked with the management group to buy one of the subsidiaries.

Additional Experience

- Executive Vice President, 1983-1987. Krug International Corporation, Dayton, Ohio.
- Executive Vice President/Director, 1979-1983 Danis Industries Corporation, Dayton, Ohio.
- President Construction Products Group, 1976-1979, Miamisburg, Ohio.
- Vice President Central Region, 1975-76.
- Materials Manager/ Purchasing Manager/Production Supervisor/MIS Development /Inventory Manager/Sales Manager/Sales Representative, 1966-75.
- Officer on active duty in the United States Marine Corps, 1963-1966.

Board Affiliations

- The CM Products Company (1984-1992), Member of the Board of Directors. Concrete Technology Inc. Springboro, Ohio (1988-89).
- Member of the Board of Directors and Chairman of the Long-Range Planning Committee.

Education

- MBA, 1968, University of Dayton
- Bachelor of Science, Personnel Management, 1963, University of Dayton

Personal

- Married, Three Sons

Rob

Education

- Ph.D., 1979, Indiana University, History of Modern Latin America
- M.S., 1967, New Mexico State University, History and Political Science
- B.A., 1965, The University of Dayton, History

Training

- Teaching Improvement Project Workshop, University of Kentucky, 1992
- Grantsmanship Training Program, The Grantsmanship Center, Columbus, Ohio, 1981
- Management Advancement Seminar, The Ohio State University, 1981
- Richard N. Bolles Career Development Seminar, Seattle, Washington, 1977
- Area Intelligence Officer Course, U.S. Army Intelligence School, Ft. Holabird, Maryland 1967-1968
- Small Group Leadership Course, U.S. Army Infantry School, Ft. Benning, Georgia, 1967

Administrative Experience

- Campus Director, Highland Heights Campus, Gateway Community College, Covington, Kentucky, 2001-2011

    Serve as chief administrator for a campus of a multi-campus community college serving Northern Kentucky. Taught history and political science. Became a full professor of History from 2006-2011 when I retired.

- Academic Dean, Jefferson Community College, Louisville, Kentucky, 2000-2002

  Serve as chief academic officer of a large urban community college. Responsible for more than 210 faculty and staff, including recruitment, evaluation, and development.

  > *Accomplishments include:*
  >
  > Hooking up the campus to an interactive television network to promote distance learning for the State of Kentucky, the United States and selected international sites.

- Vice Chancellor for Academic Affairs, Louisiana State University at Eunice, 1997-2000

  Serve as chief academic officer for a branch campus of Louisiana State University. Responsible for faculty recruitment, evaluation and development.

  > *Accomplishments include:*
  > Getting the campus into an interactive television network to promote distance learning throughout the State of Louisiana. Responsible for more than 90 faculty and staff.

- Dean of Academic Affairs, Madisonville Community College, Madisonville, Kentucky, 1990 -1997

  Serve as chief academic officer for a comprehensive community college in a predominantly rural area in southwest Kentucky. Serve as acting president in the president's absence and as the president's designee. Responsible for faculty recruitment, evaluation, and development; program development and evaluation; institutional research and strategic planning; building a distance learning program; and academic budget management. Provide leadership to an academic program in excess of 80 faculty and staff and a budget of more than seven million dollars.

Contributions and Accomplishments include:

Plan, organize, implement and lead an institutional effectiveness and strategic planning project to optimize resource development and program quality. Lead successful accreditation processes for Engineering Technology (TAC of ABET), Physical Therapist Assistant (APTA), and Nursing (NLN) programs. Lead a college-wide task force to plan and implement successfully a revamped registration and advising process that contributed to a 40% enrollment increase over a four-year period. Provide leadership in development of new programs in workforce development, community arts, adult literacy, allied health, law enforcement and engineering technology. Provide leadership for successful cooperation between college and local school district to create innovative, on-site total immersion courses and with regional school districts, vocational-technical school, and local and regional businesses and industries to promote Tech Prep and School-to-Work linkages. In cooperation with a neighboring regional university, establish an interactive compressed video television facility on campus to provide upper and graduate level interactive distance learning programming for the college's service area. Provide leadership in improving the faculty hiring process and in improving communications among the administrative divisions of the college. Promote service-learning project. Provide leadership in establishing a statewide chair development program. Work with the president in planning and solicitation of a major professional and corporate gifts capital campaign. Serve on system-wide Institutional Research Action Team.

- Associate Dean, Social Science and Humanities, North Campus, Miami-Dade Community College, Miami, Florida, 1987-1990

    Serve as the chief academic officer for the core liberal arts division of the premier campus of a large, urban, multi-campus comprehensive community college. Responsible for leadership of four academic, multidisciplinary, university-parallel departments and a preschool laboratory and child development service and training unit, including faculty and staff recruitment, evaluation, and development; overall academic planning; and budget management. Provide leadership to an academic unit with more than fifty full-time teaching faculty with a budget exceeding two million dollars.

    Contributions and Accomplishments include:

    Founding member of a multicultural task force which established a network with local public schools and universities; promotion and utilization of collegial governance; refocusing of the faculty evaluation system; capturing funds for total renovation of the campus fine arts center and faculty offices; linking the preschool laboratory unit directly to the academic education program and expanding its scope to include a joint K-2 program with the Dade County Public School District; establishing divisional and departmental planning goals and objectives; helping to achieve a six consecutive semester net gain in enrollment, reversing a twelve year decline; leading curriculum development across the division; computerizing instruction in the art and music programs; and significantly improving linkages and communications between the division and other academic and support units of the campus; and building, with department chairs, an effective management team across the division.

- Director of Community Education and Services, Southern State Community College, Hillsboro, Ohio 1985 – 1987

    Serve as the chief academic and administrative officer for the non-credit and off-campus programming for a multi-campus, rural, comprehensive community college system. Serve as chief liaison officer with local businesses and industries to develop and implement specialized workforce development training programs. Maintain a relevant, on-credit instructional program for area's businesses and industries as well as other agencies and organizations and the general public. Recruit and evaluate all faculty and staff employees by the Department of Community Education and Service and ensure completeness of records and reports to all external funding agencies, including JTPA/PIC Councils and the state departments of Education and Development. Providing general administrative leadership to the non-credit program including staff recruitment, development and evaluation and budget development and control.

    Contributions and Accomplishments include:

    Upgrading standards for the adult enrichment, continuing education, and workforce development programs, including credentialing of instructions for off-campus credit classes and establishing a professional development program for part-time non-credit faculty; planning, marketing, and co-directing an innovative summer program enrichment program for handicapped children and youth in cooperation with a local intermediate special education center and twenty one school districts; establishing and directing a comprehensive adult education and children and youths' summer enrichment program, and securing funding to begin preliminary negotiations for a student and faculty exchange program with a technical college in Brazil.

- Director of Program & Instruction, South Campus, Southern State Community College, Hillsboro, Ohio 1983 – 1985

Provide academic and administrative leadership to one campus of a multi-campus institution. Coordinate the resources of support units and staff to optimize internal efficiency and quality of instructional programs and student welfare. Maintain liaison with local community groups, agencies, and units of government to promote the interests of the college and provide meaningful educational programs relevant to the community's needs. Establish and maintain close cooperative linkages with three local universities in planning and providing graduate and advanced undergraduate courses and programs on campus. Provide essential communications links to coordinate the effectiveness of general, technical and continuing education and nursing programs. Supply overall direction on campus for faculty recruitment, evaluation, retention, and professional development. Assume direct responsibility for staff development and interdepartmental budget development and fiscal control. Provide overall supervision for liaison with community advisory committees and facilitation of curriculum development.

Contributions and Accomplishments include:

Promotion and utilization of collegial governance; revising the faculty evaluation system; establishing the weekend college; restructuring the off-campus credit program; revitalizing and expanding the foreign language program; and negotiating and coordinating a graduate educational program with a local university.

- Planning & Research Officer Southern State Community College Hillsboro, Ohio 1981-83

    In a staff position, report to and work directly with the president of the college to establish an annual and long-range planning system. Write grant proposals and facilitate a basic grants management system. Provide leadership and training to faculty in program design and grants writing techniques. Develop a system-wide faculty and staff development plan. Work with the vice-president and the academic dean in coordinating the institutional self-study for reaffirmation of accreditation. Establish and maintain a fund-raising program among area businesses and industries to include winning support grants from corporate foundations. Assist the president in lobbying at state and federal level for legislative support for higher education.

    > *Contributions and Accomplishments include:*
    >
    > Researching and writing a successful Title III proposal for enhancement of institutional planning; serving as chairman of a state-wide association of two-year colleges; being responsible for grants writing to fund a displaced/delayed entry homemaker employment program, including original staffing; and establishing and operating a federal census and general demographic data community service program over a five-county district of southwest Ohio.

- Associate Director for Planning, Highland County Community Action Organization, Hillsboro, Ohio 1978-1981

    Provide overall research, planning, and grants writing direction to a countywide human services agency with seventeen programs serving low-income and elderly individuals and families. Plan and direct a grants management system for funds in excess of $2 million from public and private sources. Provide direct leadership and supervision over four human service and educational programs. Work with the executive director in planning and conducting lobbying activities at state and federal level in support of human service programs.

Contributions and Accomplishments include:

Being solely or primarily responsible for research, project design, and writing of proposals funded in the amount of $1.5 million from public and private sources over three years' time; being solely responsible for securing grants from the state's Department of Education for innovative educational programs; restructuring the agency's outreach program and establishing and directing a joint adult basic education program in cooperation with a local college.

Teaching Experience

- Full time professor, Gateway Community College, 2006-2011
- Part-time professor, Jefferson Community College 2001-2003
- Associate professor, Madisonville Community College, *U.S. History Since 1865*, 1994-95; *Orientation to College*, 1993; Guest Lecturer for the Columbus Quincentennial Series, Humanities Division, MCC, 1992
- Associate Professor (Visiting), the University of Dayton: *History, (upper level)*, 1986
- Adjunct Faculty, Southern State Community College; *Spanish and Political Science, 1981*, 1984, 1985
- Instructor/Seminar Leader, U.S. Air Force DISAM Program, Wright Patterson Air Base, *Central American Political Culture*, 1980
- Adjunct Faculty, The University of Dayton 1978, Wright State University, 1978, Sinclair Community College, 1976, 1978

- Associate Instructor, Indiana University, *History* 1975
- Instructor, U.S. Army, Viet Nam, *Basic Intelligence Collection and ESL*, 1968
- Teaching Assistant, New Mexico State University, *History*, 1966-1967
- Instructor, Good Samaritan Hospital, Dayton, Ohio, *Basic Clinical Laboratory Procedures*, 1964

Publications/Presentations

- Co-author, *"The Educational and Economic Impact of Ohio's State-assisted Technical and Community Colleges,"* a research report of the Ohio Technical and Community College Association, 1983
- Co-author *"Retention: Organizing for Student Achievement,"* The Journal of College Student Development, March 1988
- Presenter, "A Perspective on Joseph Weizenbaum's 'On the Impact of the Computer,'" Technology and the Human Prospect Conference, The Humanities Institute, Florida State University, May 1988
- Presenter, *"Human Freedom in Aldous Huxley's Brave New World,"* The Uses and Abuses of Freedom Conference, The Humanities Institute, FSU, May 1989
- Presenter, *"The Effect of the Columbian Voyages on the New World: The Case of Mexico,"* The Columbus Quincentennial Series, Madisonville Community College, October 1992

Professional Associations

- Kentucky Association for Continuing education, 1990-2011
- National Council of Instructional Administrators, 1987-2011
- Florida Association of Community Colleges, 1987-1990
- Ohio Association of Two Year colleges, 1982 – 1987 (Board of Directors 1985-1987)
- Ohio Council for Inter-Institutional Research, 1981-1985, President, 1983-1984
- Ohio Continuing Higher Education Association, 1981-1987

- American Historical Association, 1970-2011
- Conference on Latin American History, 1970-2011
- Latin American Studies Association 1972-1984

Awards and Honors

- Honorable Order of Kentucky Colonels award from Gov. Brereton Jones for community service, 1995
- Student Government Appreciation Awards, 2001, 1991, 1984
- Exemplary Service to the Handicapped award, South Central Ohio District, Special Education Regional Resource Center, 1986
- Lincoln-Juarez Fellowship, the Mexican Department of Foreign Relations, 1973-1974
- Indiana University Graduate school Grant, 1974
- U.S. Army Commendation Medal for service in Viet Nam, 1969
- Distinguished Military Graduate, the University of Dayton, 1965

Community Service

- Member, Board of Centro de Amistad, Northern Kentucky, 2007-2011
- Member, Policy Council, United Way of Greater Cincinnati and Northern Kentucky 2006-2011
- Member of the Metro-Board, the YMCA of Greater Cincinnati 2006-2011
- Member, Board of Directors, Hopkins County Family YMCA, 1995 to present: Chairman 1997-1998
- Member, Minority Affairs Committee, Hopkins County Board of Education, 1993-2011
- Member, Curriculum Committee, Browning Springs Middle School, Madisonville, KY, 1994-1996
- Member, Kiwanis Club of Madisonville, 1993 to present: 1st Vice-President 1996-1998
- Board Member (Vice-President, 1992-1993), James Madison Days, Inc, (a civic group which produces the annual city cultural and educational festival), 1991-2011

- Member, Service Barriers Focus Group, United Way Needs Assessment Survey, and Allocation Committee, United Way, Hopkins County, Kentucky, 1991-1992
- Chairperson, Highland County (Ohio) Jail Advisory Committee, 1986-1987
- Highland County Planning Commission, 1985 Chairman, Founding Member, 1980-1987
- Board of Trustee, Scioto-Paint Valley Mental Health Center 1982-1987
- President, Highland County Pow-Wow 1982-1983
- Member, Balance-of-State CETA Planning Council, 1980-1981
- Member, CETA Regional Manpower Services Council #1, 1979-1981
- Founding Board Member, Secretary of the Board, and Membership Chairperson, Highland County Family Activities Center, 1981-1983
- Member, Highland County Head Start Policy Council, 1982 -1987

Employment History

- Campus Administrator and Professor of History, Gateway Community College 2001-2011
- Dean of Academic Affairs, Jefferson College 2000-2002
- Vice Chancellor of Academic Affairs, Louisiana State University, Eunice, 1997-2000
- Dean of Academic Affairs, Madisonville Community College, Madisonville, KY 1990-1997
- Associate Dean, Humanities and Social Sciences, Miami-Dade Community College, North Campus, Miami, Florida, 1987-1990
- System Director, Community Education and Services, Southern State Community College, Hillsboro, Ohio, 1985-1987
- Director, Program and Instruction South Campus, Southern State Community College, 1983-1985
- Interim Director of Student Services, South Campus Southern State Community College, 1982

- Planning, Research, and Development Officer, Southern State Community College 1981-1983
- Associate Director for Planning, Highland County Community Action Organization, Hillsboro, Ohio, 1978-1981
- Senior Counselor and Satellite Director, Counseling Services Northwest, Seattle, Washington, 1976-1977
- Associate Instructor and Research Assistant, Department of History, Indiana University, 1974-75
- Residence Life Counselor, student Services, Indiana University, 1969-1972
- Intelligence Officer, U.S. Army, Continental U.S. and the Republic of South Viet Nam, 1967-1969
- Graduate Assistant, Department of History and Social Science, New Mexico State University, Las Cruces, N.M., 1965-1967
- Clinical Laboratory Technician, Instructor and systems Analyst, Good Samaritan hospital, Dayton, Ohio, 1961-1965, summer, 1969

Personal

- Two children, good health
- Hobbies include music, running, handball, gardening and landscaping, reading, personal computers, and general aviation.

Chris

Professional Activities

- As a member of the CHSRA team, utilized professional knowledge in the areas of nursing and regulations to assist with the development of a revised Long-Term Care Survey Process.
- Monitored the facilities of two Long Term Care Corporations to assure quality care in compliance with an agreement with the Office of Inspector General
- Evaluated surveyors in the field, as a supervisor in the Colorado State survey Agency to assure consistency and quality of the long-term care survey process.
- Supervised teams of long-term care surveyors, evaluating their performance, planning schedules and providing guidance. Trained providers and survey staff employees on issues related to long-term care and the survey process. Coordinate state survey activities with the Federal regional office.
- For two years chaired a committee of professionals working to determine best facility practices to deal with residents with behavioral difficulties in long term care settings.
- Certified to survey long term care, home health agencies and hospitals.

Employment History

- Researcher & Analyst, CHRSA and Long-Term Care Institute, University of Wisconsin Madison, Wisconsin, November 2001 to 2008

- Clinical Field Supervisor, Colorado Department of Public Health and Environment Denver, Colorado, September 1999 to November 2001
- Nurse Consultant, Pinion Management Company Denver, Colorado, November 1998 to July 1999
- Long Term Care Supervisor, Colorado Department of Public Health and Environment Denver, Colorado, September 1995 to February 1998
- Long Term Care and Hospital Surveyor, Colorado Department of Public Health and Environment, Denver, Colorado, December 1989 to February 1998

Education:
- Master of Arts, with honors, Community Health University of Northern Colorado. Greeley, Colorado. August 1987
- Bachelors of Arts in Sociology, with honors, University of Colorado. Boulder, Colorado. June 1983
- Diploma, with honors, Nursing Good Samaritan Hospital School of Nursing. School President. Dayton, Ohio. June 1966

Paula

Education
- Bachelors of Arts in English and Journalism, Murray State

Employment
- Denver Post

Honors
- "Volunteer of the Year" at Gonzaga Prep High School

Personal
- Birthdate: August 1, 1948
- Married: June 12, 1976 in Longmont, Colorado to Robert Cooper
- 3 Children: Andrew, Haley, and Catherine
- Hobbies, Interests: Quilting, needlepoint, travel, volunteerism at her children's schools

Beth

Summary of Qualifications:

- 35 years of library reference experience in academic, public and research libraries
- 12 years of successful supervisory experience, 12 years as a staff member of Clark State, working closely with students, staff, faculty, administrators and members of the community
- Keen understanding of and appreciation for the mission and academic programs at Clark State
- Consistently recognized by supervisors for outstanding customer service skills
- Advanced research database searching skill
- Extensive collection development experience in academic and research libraries
- Successful library user training, program planning, and classroom teaching experience
- Authored three successful grant proposals to purchase over $10,000 of library materials
- Presented at national and state conferences regarding internet resources

Current Work Experience:

- Clark State Community College, Springfield, OH. July 2003–2016

    Director of Library Services. July 2011–2016

    - Developed new promotional materials for the library, requested and granted upgrades for two

library staff positions, reorganized acquisitions procedures to better support academic programming, initiated and oversaw the reorganization of the physical layout of book collection, completed a SWOT analysis with staff that is being used as a planning tool, encouraged broader staff participation in campus-wide events and professional development opportunities, reorganized the library work room to better utilize the space for processing archives and OhioLINK requests, completed three successful "Staff and Faculty Favorites" reading initiatives, reintroduced the hiring of college work study students and successfully petitioned for major upgrades to the lighting in library study areas.
- Oversaw the reorganization of College Archives, visited selected two-year colleges to observe their models for branch libraries, completing a proposal for library services at Greene Center and Bellefontaine, introduced a monthly "New Titles List" page to website, hired a new Technical Services and Systems Librarian, extensively weeded the collection to create space for new study/collaboration space.
- Upgraded the library's website, incorporating more e-books and other new electronic materials to the collection, introduced LibGuides to our Web page, upgraded the library systems software and secured them behind the proper firewalls, migrated the integrated library system from Millennium to the Sierra software from Innovative Interfaces Inc.

Career Specialist/Adjunct Instructor, Office of Career Management, August 2006 – June 2011
- Assisted students with career planning and assessment, resume writing, interviewing, and coordinating co-op and internships. Coordinated campus-wide job fairs, professional development luncheons, co-op placement and acted as Interim

Director for 4 months. Taught employability skills related workshops and a credit course. Elected by peers to the CSCC Staff Senate and served on the President's Diversity Council. Awarded a $2300 grant from the Diversity Council to purchase library materials on Diversity in the Workplace."

Registrar, Records & Registration, July 2003- August 2006

- Supervised a permanent staff of four and numerous work-study students. Responsible for the maintenance and security of all student records. Simultaneously acted as the Ohio Residency Officer, Veterans Services Representative and International Student Advisor.

Related Library Experience

- Reference Librarian, Chicago Botanic Garden, June Price Reedy Library, Glencoe, IL, November 2000 – June 2003

    Provided specialized reference services and library instruction to the staff, garden members, and administrators of the Botanic Garden as well as to the general public, visiting scholars and students.

    Expanded the scope of the collection in many areas especially in reference, children's, teachers curriculum materials, and horticultural therapy

    Expanded reference services, particularly to the garden's research staff and reintroduced mediated bibliographic database searching.

    Revamped and streamlined inter-library loan procedures, reorganized the serials collection, and initiated a binding program for serials.

    Acted as the supervisor of the library's volunteers and organized an annual "Appreciation Day" event for the Library's 30+ volunteers.

- Reference Librarian, Kansas State University, Hale Library, Manhattan, KS, August 1994 – October 2000

    Served mainly in the Science Library as a reference librarian and bibliographer.

    Acted as a liaison and bibliographic instructor to students and faculty in the electrical, civil and agricultural engineering, geology, and horticulture departments.

    Supervised student assistants in the Science Library on evenings and weekends. Coordinated collection development and maintenance of the print reference collection.

    Briefly served as Interim Reference Coordinator for the Science Library and was elected by my peers to the KSU Faculty Senate.

    Appointed by the Dean of the Engineering School to serve on the design team for the Engineering Library.

    Awarded two grants by the Kansas Library Network Interlibrary Loan Development Program to purchase library materials on "Children's Gardening" ($4000) and "Horticulture Therapy" ($4400)

- Engineering/Science Librarian, Sears Library, Case Western Reserve University, Cleveland OH, January 1990 – July 1994

    Provided a wide range of information services to faculty and students in a large academic library. Acted as the liaison to the geological sciences, math, and the biomedical, civil, and electrical engineering departments.

    Hired, trained and supervised two library assistants and two student assistants. Successfully interviewed a large cross section of students and faculty to solicit their input for the design of the Kelvin Smith Library.

- Reference Librarian, Law Library, Sears Library, Case Western Reserve University, Cleveland OH, Summer 1987, and June 1989 – December 1989

    Provided extensive research assistance to faculty, students, and the general public in a large academic law library.

    Assisted with library user instruction, database searching, government publications, and collection development.

- Reference Librarian Ursuline College Ralph Besse Library, Cleveland, OH, September 1987 – May 1989

    Coordinated and promoted all reference services, including library user instruction, database searching and collection development.

    Supervised interlibrary loan and served as library supervisor in the absence of the Library Director.

- Manager, Information Services Merrick & Co., Denver, CO, April 1984 - May 1986

    Served as the Library/Records Manager for a large engineering/architectural consulting firm.

    Reorganized and expanded the company's library facility and established an active job records program; compiled the company's library/records policy manual; revised index to company records and drawings; initiated a forms management program; and provided in-depth library reference services to architects and engineers. Maintained the company's specification files and architectural product samples collection. Supervised two part-time assistants.

    Co-founded the Engineering Information Network, a consortium of Denver area consulting engineering librarians.

Worked as a cartographic Technician in 1974 and returned to the company after graduate school as the corporate librarian in 1984.

- Corporate Librarian, URS Company, Denver, CO, 1981- April 1984

    Provided extensive library research and reference services to 75 engineers, architects, planners, and environmental scientists. Designed and organized the physical layout of the library.

    Managed all cataloging, acquisitions and budget related tasks. Supervised two temporary librarians hired to assist with cataloging the book collection. Networked extensively with science and engineering librarians in local federal, public and academic libraries.

- Senior Librarian, Government Publications Division, Denver Public Library, Denver CO, 1978 – 1981

    Provided reference assistance to patrons including state legislators, university professors and students, and members of the general public with United Nation, U.S. Federal, Colorado and Denver documents.

- Project Leader, Fish & Wildlife Reference Service

    Managed a bibliographic database related to wildlife management under a multi-year contract between the U.S. Fish & Wildlife Service and the Denver Public Library.

    Supervised a staff of five that indexed and distributed research reports to wildlife biologists throughout the United States.

- Reference Librarian, Arapahoe Regional Library District, Littleton, CO, 1976 – 1978

    Totally reorganized, designed, and supervised the reference department, and assisted with adult program planning and nonfiction collection development.

- Librarian 1-A Dayton Metro Library, Dayton, OH, 1972 – 1973 & 1975

    Responsible for reference assistance and collection development in the Social Sciences Department of the Main Library. (Left to attend Library School at the University of Denver)

Education

- Kansas State University: Manhattan, KS
  Completed 50+ hours toward a B.S. in Horticulture 3.97 G.P.A.; Member of the honors society for the College of Agriculture
- University of Denver: Denver, CO
  M.A. in Librarianship
- Bowling Green State University; Bowling Green, OH
  B.S. in Secondary Education, geography major and library science minor

Phil

Early Employment

- Newspaper routes
- Coca cola plant
- Rike's Department Store
- AAA
- Siebenthaler's Nursery
- Dayton Daily News truck driver
- Telemarketer

Permanent Employment

- United States Post Office, 1981- November 2012

Awards

- MVP Little League
- Lettered in tennis
- Dean's list junior year of college
- USPS – Safe Driver
- USPS – Mailman Extraordinaire 2005

Personal

- Birthdate November 4, 1955
- Hobbies include Cub Scouts, Boy Scouts, Explorers; half marathons; swimming – almost daily at present; gardening; reading presidential biographies, financial management

Doug

Summary

- Experienced salesperson with extraordinary customer service skill and positive attitude seeking challenging sales position

Skills

- Knowledge and training in SAP, CRM and MS Office Software

Professional Work Experience

- Panini Company – inside channel manager – bank check scanners – 2016 to present
- Kronecranes – overhead inside cranes for factories - Account Manager- 2013-2016
- C2G – Cables to Go/Lastar Inc., Moraine, Ohio   July 2003 – March 2013

Technical Sales Representative

- Led in calls taken, time available and total talk time among all Call Center employees.
- Developed strong customer relationships and was recognized as a leader in department for offering solutions.
- Successfully assisted National Account Managers and all AM's in the OEM and VAO divisions with PO processing, quotes, RMA's customer service issues and follow up.
- Managed sales via telephone, instant messaging and inbound customer emails.

- Assisted with training new employees.
- Excelled at resolving customer complaints regarding sales and service.
- Revised and updated key procedures for sales departments.
- Contributed positively to Net Promoter Scores.

Account Manager July 2003 - July 2008

- Attained 100% plus quota for three out of five years.
- Successfully built and maintained customer relationships throughout bound and inbound calls, emails and onsite visits.
- Developed excellent follow-up skills for optimal customer satisfaction.
- Targeted sales to corporate, government, and educational customers.
- Efficiently processed custom and stock orders, quotes, returns, and credits.
- Serviced up to 500 accounts and supported other account managers as needed

Global Computer/Infotel, Fletcher, Ohio June 1999 – July 2003

Network Sales Specialist/Account Manager

- Sold network-related products to corporate, government, education and reseller accounts.
- Assisted in network sales to over 300 sales representatives nationwide.
- Led the networking department in calls taken and talk time every year.

Education

- Bachelors of Science in Marketing, Wright State University, Dayton, Ohio

ABOUT THE AUTHOR

The author was born in Dayton, Ohio, as our country was leaving the Great Depression and entering World War II. It was a time of economic vibrancy, strong cultural identity and general optimism. Twenty-one years later, Grant had seven siblings, many stories, and a place in the freshman class of medical school. After training in Internal Medicine at Mayo Clinic Rochester, Minnesota, he served his military duty as a Captain at Fairchild Air Force Base hospital in Spokane, Washington. He chose Bellingham, Washington for his life's work. Family fun with six children, mountain climbing, racketball, and some medical writing were squeezed into a busy life. Retirement gave opportunity to travel, sing in chorales, and write this book. He and his wife Candice spend their winters in Arizona.

www.ingramcontent.com/pod-product-compliance
Lightning Source LLC
Chambersburg PA
CBHW062057290426
44110CB00022B/2619